MW00586247

PHILOSOPHY as POETRY

PAGE-BARBOUR
LECTURES
for 2004

PHILOSOPHY as POETRY

RICHARD RORTY

UNIVERSITY *of* VIRGINIA PRESS

Charlottesville & London

University of Virginia Press
© 2016 by the Rector and Visitors of the University of Virginia
All rights reserved
Printed in the United States of America on acid-free paper

First published 2016
ISBN 978-0-8139-3933-9 (cloth)
ISBN 978-0-8139-3934-6 (e-book)

9 8 7 6 5 4 3

Library of Congress Cataloging-in-Publication Data

Names: Rorty, Richard, author.
Title: Philosophy as poetry / Richard Rorty.
Description: Charlottesville : University of Virginia Press, 2016.
Series: Page-Barbour lectures for 2004 | Includes index.
Identifiers: LCCN 2016022491| ISBN 9780813939339 (cloth :
alk. paper) | ISBN 9780813939346 (e-book)
Subjects: LCSH: Philosophy, American—20th century. | Rorty,
Richard.
Classification: LCC B945.R523 P44 2016 | DDC 191—dc23
LC record available at https://lccn.loc.gov/2016022491

Jacket photo: Steve Pyke/Getty Images

CONTENTS

INTRODUCTION: *The Assent of Man*
   Michael Bérubé   vii

1 Getting Rid of the Appearance-Reality
     Distinction   1

2 Universalist Grandeur and
     Analytic Philosophy   23

3 Romanticism, Narrative Philosophy,
     and Human Finitude   43

AFTERWORD
     Mary V. Rorty   63

INDEX   67

INTRODUCTION

The Assent of Man

MICHAEL BÉRUBÉ

THE THREE PAGE-BARBOUR LECTURES THAT MAKE UP *Philosophy as Poetry* mount an argument that will come as no surprise to people familiar with the work of Richard Rorty; but by the same token, they offer a useful introduction to his distinctive form of American pragmatism. If you are trying to understand why Rorty was as influential and as controversial as he was, these lectures are a very good place to start. Rorty was often considered—especially by critics outside the world of academe—to be one of those postmodernist-nihilist-antifoundationalist-poststructuralist-sophist-relativists who corrupt our youth and whose success offers right-thinking people a barometer of the intellectual decline of the American university. (This sentence should properly be concluded with a loud *harrumph.*) But unlike most post-this-or-that philosophers, Rorty wrote in the plain style, free of technical language and clever neologisms, and remained determinedly optimistic about vanilla liberal democracy; indeed, Rorty believed that postmodernists and poststructuralists were on the wrong track—that they were right to reject the idea that philosophy should appeal to something external to human experience in its search for "Truth," but wrong to reject the liberal pragmatism that tries, however modestly, to make life a little better for people if it can.

In these pages, then, you will read that it is a mistake to think of philosophy as the search for access to, and objective knowledge about, the transcendent and the ineffable. And you will be advised that it is a "mistake" not in the sense that such access and knowledge do not correspond to the way things-in-themselves really are (for that would be still more Platonism, dividing false appearances from real reality), but in the sense that the pursuit of such access and knowledge leads only to annoying headaches and the fruitless generation of philosophical pseudoproblems. So if you are already familiar with this terrain, the argument itself is not a surprise; it is not as if we have searched through Richard Rorty's papers and found the anomalous series of lectures that throws our understanding of his career into crisis, the lectures that insist that philosophy should, if practiced properly, produce objective knowledge about the ineffable. It is, however, something of a surprise that *this* iteration of the argument has not, until now, seen the light of day—with its beavers, mud, and sticks (in the first lecture) and with its insistence (throughout) that language, and human thought, begins only when one grunter of sounds can rationally assent to or criticize the sounds of a fellow grunter. I will say more about those aspects of the argument below—the beavers and the grunting, or meta-grunting, and the importance of assent—for both are important to how Rorty understands human intelligence, the prospects for human life, and the limitations of human finitude. I will also offer a reading of Rorty's rhetoric, his habitual and canny framing of his arguments in terms of what we will have appreciated about them once they have become part of ordinary human common sense. I want to open, however, by telling a story about surprises in the archives.

It was May 2010, and the occasion was a one-day conference at the University of California, Irvine, organized to mark the opening of the Richard Rorty Papers in the UC Irvine Libraries Critical Theory Archive. The conference was convened by Liz Losh and was titled, after one of Rorty's catchier aphorisms, "Time Will Tell, but Epistemology Won't." I decided to show up a day early and spend some hours leafing through the archives, just to see what I could see. I had been Rorty's student once, twenty-five years earlier, and he had served on my dissertation committee as the "outside" reader (that is, the reader outside the English department), but I did not know him well as a person. I saw some useful things, including this very Rortyan passage from a 1998 lecture titled "How Relevant Is 'Postmodern' Philosophy to Politics?": "We shall only get the full benefit of either Hegelian historicism or pragmatist anti-representationalism when we have become as insouciant about the question 'did human beings have intrinsic dignity, and human rights, before anybody thought they did?' as we are about the question 'did transfinite cardinal numbers exist before Cantor found a way to talk about them?'"

That will be a good day—or, more precisely, we will have realized, after that day comes, that it was a good day. And I was so pleased at having found this distilled quintessence of Rortyism that I decided to stop reading Rorty's unpublished lectures and look instead at some of Rorty's correspondence, just out of curiosity.

There were many things I was not surprised to find: a letter to Frederick Crews, complaining about people who take physics as the paradigmatic form of human knowledge and think that philosophy should aspire to be a kind of epistemological physics; a heartbreaking letter from Harold Bloom touching on various personal matters; routine professional correspondence, letters of recommendation, and so forth. I wasn't surprised to see my correspondence with Rorty from 1994–95, which consists of a series of letters about my second book, *Public Access,* in which Rorty chastised me for my dismissive attitude toward social democrats like Irving Howe and Arthur Schlesinger Jr., and I insisted in response that Schlesinger's *The Disuniting of America,* like Richard Bernstein's *Dictatorship of Virtue,* was a hysterical book, devoted to the proposition that "multiculturalism" would eat away at the very fabric of American society. It was nice to see that exchange in its very own subfolder, but I remembered it well, and so moved on to . . .

A most curious artifact. Three sheets of yellow legal paper, covered with what appeared to be my handwriting. No, let me not fall back into the appearance-reality distinction: it *was* my handwriting. The letter was dated June 23, 1985, and it was basically an agonized request for an extension on my overdue paper. I have no idea why Rorty kept it, but reading it was genuinely *unheimlich,* as if I had been granted access to a parallel universe and allowed to revisit my much younger self. The situation was this: after taking Rorty's Heidegger seminar that spring, I had the option of taking a final exam or writing a stand-alone paper. The exam was by far the easier option, and one of the questions, "To what extent does part 1 of *Being and Time* advance a pragmatist theory of truth?," was an implicit invitation to go over our notes from the first four weeks of class and say, "Well, it pretty much does, just like Rorty says it does." I didn't want to do that, because I thought I had my own little take on part 1 of *Being and Time.* But I wasn't sure how to go about writing it down.

At that point, at the end of my second year in graduate school, I was in dangerous territory. I had a late paper hanging over my head, and worse, it was a late paper for a famous and distinguished professor. I was twenty-three years old. I was not a student of philosophy. And I was quite convinced that there was nothing I could put into a paper on Martin Heidegger that would be of any interest to Rorty whatsoever. Week by week that conviction deepened, as did my sense of dread. So in June, just before Rorty left for a trip to China, I clenched my teeth, steeled my nerve, and sat down to write a letter (*a*) sketching out my idea and (*b*) asking for an extension.

Dear reader, surely you are familiar with the genre of letter I wrote: crazed, anxious, writing-blocked graduate student expounds on the details of a potentially promising but never-to-be-written essay. The first two and a half pages walked through the half-formed argument, in which I suggested that what Rorty took to be the "pragmatist" aspects of *Being and Time* (the categories of the *vorhanden* and *zuhanden,* or "present-at-hand" and "ready-to-hand") are just setups for the real payload, the insistence that "truth" is a matter of "disclosure" (*aletheia*), and that one of the reasons Heidegger goes to such trouble to establish those categories is to persuade us that factual assertions, far from being the locus of truth, are merely present-at-hand entities that get stuff done. This may sound like a pragmatist critique of positivism (which is no doubt why Rorty liked it), but it's not where Heidegger leaves the argument; in sections 43 and 44, he insists that since assertions are not the locus of truth, as he has conclusively demonstrated, truth must be something else, namely, the disclosure of Being specific to *Dasein*. *Dasein* was Heidegger's word (literally, "being-there") for human sentience, the form of existence and awareness we bring to the world into which we are thrown ("thrown-ness" being another key early Heideggerism, like "being-with-others").

Being with a capital *B,* for Heidegger, must be distinguished from mere beings, and to grasp that distinction, in *Being and Time,* we need also to distinguish truth-as-disclosure from mere assertions about things.

This much is probably obvious to anyone familiar with Heidegger, but I was twenty-three and just feeling my way around the most difficult book I had ever read. The tricky part—the part on which I was stuck—lay in the realization that I was more or less saying that part 1 of *Being and Time* involves an elaborate performative contradiction whereby Heidegger argues logically and patiently (and laboriously, good lord) that argument is not where truth lives. I had the glimmer of an idea that perhaps this might shed some light on the famous "turn," which, on my reading, might have amounted to Heidegger saying (among other things), "You know, I'm not going to argue anymore that assertions are merely present-at-hand. I'm just going to go straight to *aletheia* and disclosure, and write sweeping accounts of philosophy since the pre-Socratics, meditations on romantic poets such as Friedrich Hölderlin and the phrase 'it gives being,' and a bunch of stuff about the clearing and the jug and the fourfold, so there." If life had not intervened, my paper probably would remain unwritten to this day (with the world so much the poorer for it). More important to me, had I not written that paper, I doubt very much that I would have completed my Ph.D. But I did write it in late August, and even though I did not keep a copy of the letter I had written to Rorty in June, I somehow managed to follow precisely the plan I had laid out (though I did not realize this until I consulted the archives in 2010).

The reason I finally wrote the paper was quite simple: in the middle of August of that year, my girlfriend informed me that she was pregnant. My first thought was *Oh my goodness, we're going to get married and we're going to be parents;* my second thought, milliseconds later, was *Oh my goodness, if we're going to have a baby, I need to finish that damn Rorty paper.* My anxiety about the-being-that-would-become-Nicholas Bérubé quashed all my anxiety about the-being-that-was-the-paper-I-could-not-write, and I wrote the essay in a frenzy over four or five days. It turned out to be the last paper I would ever write out longhand before typing. And it turned out, when I finally finished typing, to be fifty pages. After stewing over the essay for months and months, I had become the Graduate Student from Hell, turning in my paper very late and very long.

If you are a graduate student, *do not do this.* It is a very, very bad thing to do.

But it was a formative experience. Not only because it got me off the schneid with regard to *Being and Time,* but because it taught me how to manage academic anxieties: that is, by using serious ones to dissolve more trivial ones. "Merciful Moloch, we're going to have a baby, so I have to finish this class so that I can finish my coursework so that I can write my dissertation and try to get a job" is so much weightier than "What if Rorty doesn't like/is bored by/disagrees with my essay" that there's no point wasting any time with the latter.

Still, I could not believe Rorty kept that letter. I recognized the kid who wrote it, a leaner and squirrelier version of the person who's writing this essay, but beyond that, I remembered that whole weird and directionless Charlottesville summer, working every day at the National Legal Research Group to pay the rent, not writing, breaking up my band (and then recording a posthumous album anyway), wondering whether I should even stay in graduate school, wondering whether I could.

And twenty-five years later, there I was in the Rorty papers, not only reliving that summer of doubt and anxiety but learning, at long last, what Rorty really thought of my Heidegger paper. He had returned it to me within a month, because he was a *mensch* and (as all his colleagues have testified) a voracious and deeply diligent reader of everything, but he said little more than *This is a convincing reading and I don't have any interesting criticisms of it.* In the archives, however, I found a letter of recommendation in which Rorty called the essay "one of the best papers on Heidegger I have ever received from a graduate student" and remarked that "the paper made me rethink a lot of my own views on early Heidegger." By this I was totally and very pleasantly surprised. And then I winced at this passage: "On the basis of his participation in seminar discussion, I had expected a good paper from Berube, but I had not expected him to throw himself so whole-heartedly into Heidegger and to write fifty pages of close and detailed analysis. (He could just as easily have earned his 'A' by writing fifteen pages, and by reading only the assigned passages, instead of spending months on the project.)" Goddamn. I had to wait twenty-five years to hear that.

There's a lesson here, I suspect. The lesson is that you never know what's going to wind up in the archives. Even your crazed letter, "Dear Professor Rorty, can I have an extension because the dog ate my *vorhanden* and I stayed up late being-with-others and overslept and I promise to turn in my paper precisely when I finish it which should be any day now sincerely yours," might be in there, somewhere, for scholars of the future to marvel at. Suffice it to say that the lectures collected here are somewhat more important documents than my handwritten letter from June 1985. And it is still a surprise to read them in 2016.

I had not planned on taking a Heidegger seminar with Rorty at all. In the fall of 1984, I decided it was high time I learned something about the world of contemporary literary theory, and I had heard that Rorty would be offering a seminar on Derrida in the fall of 1985. But I was advised to take the upcoming Heidegger seminar instead. "If you want to understand where all this poststructuralism comes from," I was told, "you can't do better than to start with Rorty on Heidegger." That was exceptionally good advice. The Heidegger seminar introduced me to the contingency of value and the wonders of late Wittgenstein, but not because Rorty converted me to the philosophy of Heidegger himself; Rorty did not teach that way, in the manner of a disciple, which may be one reason why he was so influential without generating disciples of his own. Unlike Heidegger and Derrida, he was not iconic, and did what he could to resist iconicity. At the time, Rorty was mainly interested in Heidegger's work on the history of Western philosophy. Rorty responded most fully to the first half of Heidegger's career, in which Heidegger could be plausibly aligned with the American pragmatism that Heidegger despised and Rorty revered. That was the reason for his interest in the *Vorhandensein* and the *Zuhandensein:* inasmuch as Heidegger construed objects and assertions about objects as mere "ready-to-hand" and "present-at-hand" tools, Rorty thought he was worth aligning with Dewey and anyone else who is willing to see philosophical debates as forms of problem-solving, no different in kind from questions that carpenters and plumbers and physicists pose to themselves whenever they are confronted with difficult tasks.

As the semester progressed, it became clear that Rorty thought of Heidegger's idea of *aletheia*-as-truth as an anticipation, written in dense German neologisms, of Thomas Kuhn's argument about paradigm change in *The Structure of Scientific Revolutions:* the paradigm shifts were the "disclosures," and the consequent research programs were full of present-at-hand assertions about the objects made available to us by those disclosures. (A version of that argument appears in the first lecture, when Rorty suggests that "getting the word 'red' into circulation was a feat on a par with Newton's persuading people to use the term 'gravity.'") For Heidegger's late work Rorty had almost no use at all, and was happy to let fans of late Heidegger elaborate on the elusive nature of *Ereignis* while he comically furrowed his brow, sighed, and shrugged his shoulders.

Throughout the seminar, Rorty generously gave us copies of his essays-in-progress as he was establishing the lines of thought that led to his 1989 book *Contingency, Irony, and Solidarity;* he also gave us copies of essays written by people who disagreed with him passionately. John Caputo, for instance, lit into Rorty's indifference to late Heidegger, charging that "Rorty denies the strangest of the strange in Heidegger, the abiding incommensurability of the thought which thinks that which is not a thing," and capping off the indictment with the accusation that all Rorty really wanted was for the discipline of philosophy to keep a civil conversation going. "Well, he's got me there," Rorty admitted ingenuously, furrowing his brow and looking around at the class. "That really *is* all I want."

It was the signature Rorty gesture, at once disarming and vexing. On the one hand, it took the *agon* of debate down a few notches: when you're arguing with someone who says he simply wants to keep a civil conversation going, you run the risk of sounding insufferably pompous if you insist, *No, can't you see, there's something much larger at stake here.* On the other hand, what if there *is* something much larger at stake here?

There were moments that spring when I felt as if Rorty was trying to cure us of our infatuation with the numinous and inviting us instead to live in a world where there was nothing more profound than zoning laws and recycling centers. And then there were moments—many more of them, in the end—when I believed that this invitation was a good thing, that philosophy is better off without the damn numinous already and should pay attention to the quotidian and the sublunary. So far as I know, Rorty never said much about zoning laws and recycling centers. But to everyone who insisted that a man's reach should exceed his grasp, that there was something Out There to which we should aspire and to which our thoughts and beliefs should correspond, Rorty would reply, in effect, *Yes, that's what a heaven's for. But I prefer to think about our lives right here on Earth.*

I wound up not taking Rorty's Derrida seminar in the fall of 1985 after all—or his Freud seminar the semester after that. But the graduate-student gossip about those later courses was intense: whereas there were no True Believers in the Heidegger seminar, the Derrida and Freud courses were populated by graduate students and practicing psychoanalysts who were convinced that Derrida and Freud were not merely interesting intellectual figures who wrote intriguing things but revealers of the One True Path to Human Enlightenment (or post-Enlightenment). Predictably, these people were infuriated by what they saw as Rorty's irreverent attitude toward their icons, and toward iconicity.

Rorty infuriated many True Believers in the course of his career; for many years he was considered an apostate by Anglo-American analytic philosophers, or as someone who had simply stopped doing real philosophy. I don't want to exaggerate the degree of Rorty's alienation from the world of professional philosophy; he was a more complex figure than that, and he somehow managed to think in the analytic and the Continental traditions at the same time: he continued to talk of Quine and Habermas, Davidson and Foucault, Carnap and Derrida long after most people had pledged allegiance to one side or the other. Yet the history of his academic appointments nonetheless forms a kind of triptych, a *Rorty's Progress* from philosophy at Princeton to the humanities at Virginia to comparative literature at Stanford, where, as James Ryerson noted, in a very fine postmortem on Rorty's career, he "twitt[ed] his own popularity by suggesting that his title be 'transitory professor of trendy studies.'" Still, Rorty wasn't fully embraced by the proponents of theory, either; his shoulder-shrugging treatment of deconstruction and psychoanalysis as possible "vocabularies" (rather than as a set of true propositions about language and the unconscious) seemed deliberately to cultivate an air of intellectual insouciance— the kind of insouciance with which Rorty wanted us to dismiss the question of whether there *really are* such things as human dignity and human rights. At a time when Jacques Derrida was being hailed as the man who had decisively won the Continental tradition's Last Philosopher Standing competition (Derrida overcoming the last vestiges of Platonic logocentrism in Heidegger after Heidegger had overcome the last vestiges of "inverted" Platonism in Nietzsche after Nietzsche had overcome the last vestiges of Platonism in everybody else), Rorty was content to see Derrida's work as an interesting kind of writing—almost as if Derrida were a figure more like James Joyce than like John Rawls. Which, in the end, is an entirely reasonable way to read Derrida.

The Theory Wars of the 1980s were a great and terrible thing. Who knows how many lives were lost in the struggle between humanism and posthumanism, belletrism and barbaric jargon, New Criticism and newer criticism? When I arrived at the University of Virginia in 1983, deconstruction had already peaked at Yale—but the Battle of Charlottesville was just beginning. The arguments between pro-theory and anti-theory people were not particularly interesting. There was too much fuddy-duddyism on the anti-theory side, too much intellectual narrowness among people who just wanted to keep teaching their literature classes without all this wrangling over things like contingency and indeterminacy. But the arguments between theorists were fascinating. One of those arguments was staged precisely *as* a contest, as a kind of showdown: Rorty versus E. D. Hirsch on the determinacy of meaning. All the graduate students looked forward to it—it was our equivalent of Ali-Frazier. And who knew? Perhaps it would finally determine whether meaning was determinate, once and for all.

This was just before Hirsch became the head of Cultural Literacy Enterprises, back when his main claim to fame was *Validity in Interpretation,* the lonely outpost from which he kept careful watch over what he saw as the actual intentions of authors. By the time he arrived for the Determinacy Debate, however, he had modified his original position considerably, and he said so. Now, he was no longer willing to insist that "meaning" consists only of those interpretations that accord with the intentions of a writer or a speaker. At the time, we students speculated that perhaps the reductio of this position, that meaning is simply identical with intention, which had recently been proposed in all seriousness by Steven Knapp and Walter Benn Michaels in "Against Theory," led Hirsch to back away from it cautiously. But he still wanted people to agree that there is a difference between meanings that accord with a speaker/writer's intentions and meanings that do not. His terms, of course, were "validity" (for intentionalist interpretations) and "significance" (for everything else). And he wanted us to agree that the people seated at the Validity Table were doing one kind of literary criticism and theory, and that all the people at the various Significance Tables were doing other kinds of literary criticism and theory.

I was ridiculously eager to hear Rorty's response. Hirsch's argument seemed like the kind of thing that badly needed dismantling, and I figured Rorty was just the guy to do it. Surely he would reach back into his store of arguments from analytical philosophy, the arguments he once believed and now repudiated, to show why the validity-significance distinction is neither coherent nor useful. Surely he would show us all, decisively, that meaning is indeterminate. But he did no such thing. Instead, he simply replied, "I don't know, Don. I guess you care what the field of literary criticism looks like fifty years from now, and I just don't."

I admit that I was disappointed. It seemed to me, at the time, that Rorty had leapfrogged over three or four necessary stages of argument in order to go right to the metaquestion of what the future of the field might conceivably look like. But now I know that in his deliberately offhand, insouciant way, Rorty was asking about the stakes of the debate itself— indeed, the stakes of any debate. Is the purpose of the debate to nail something down once and for all, marking the terrain that need not be debated any longer? Or is it a mistake, in such matters, to think that something can be nailed down once and for all? Is it better to leave it to our descendants to determine for themselves whether they want to think of meaning as determinate or indeterminate? Rorty, in that debate as in these lectures, emphatically cast his lot with option (b): Let's not try to nail things down. Let's try instead to keep a civil conversation going. And let's try to keep things interesting: as Rorty puts it in his second lecture here, "Universalist Grandeur and Analytic Philosophy," "Whereas Frege and Russell hoped to make things clearer, Hegel and Heidegger hoped to make things different." This openness to novelty made it possible for Rorty to enjoy Derrida and Heidegger as interesting writers. And if you objected, "Yes, but he enjoyed Derrida and Heidegger as interesting writers and nothing more," Rorty may very well have replied that they did not need to be anything more. "Narrative philosophers," he writes at the outset of the third lecture here, "Romanticism, Narrative Philosophy, and Human Finitude," "agree with Wittgenstein that there are no meanings of words to be analyzed, but only uses of words to be described—uses that are, and should be, in constant change. There are no universal and necessary truths to be discovered, but only social practices to be accepted or rejected." That, I like to imagine, is Rorty's longer reply to E. D. Hirsch on the determinacy of meaning.

In one of his great elegies, "In Memory of Sigmund Freud," Auden wrote:

> For every day they die
> among us, those who were doing us some good,
> who knew it was never enough but
> hoped to improve a little by living.

When Rorty died in 2007, I immediately thought of those lines. By that time, I had come to believe that there was something deeply paradoxical at work in Rorty's political and philosophical life. Over the course of Rorty's career, it became ever clearer that, despite his demurrals about the importance of philosophy and his agnosticism about the relation of philosophy to politics, Rorty *did* believe—or, at the very least, hope—that the world would become at once more secular and more pragmatist, and that it would do so for the same reasons. The paradox, then, is this: even as Rorty continued to insist that the disputes of professional philosophers don't determine the fate of the world, he showed us why they might matter—provided that we can stop thinking of philosophy as the search for Objective Truth and begin thinking of it instead as a creative enterprise of dreaming up new and more humane ways to live.

These lectures open, appropriately, with that hope: if we can just drop the distinction between appearance and reality, which, for Rorty, has "outlived whatever usefulness it may have had" (note, again, that it is not *wrong,* for that too would be a claim about how things really are),

> we should no longer wonder whether the human mind, or human language, is capable of representing reality accurately. We would stop thinking that some parts of our culture are more in touch with reality than other parts. We would express our sense of finitude not by comparing our humanity with something nonhuman but by comparing our way of being human with other, better, ways that may someday be adopted by our descendants. When we condescended to our ancestors, we would not say that they were less in touch with reality than we are, but that their imaginations were more limited than ours. We would boast of being able to talk about more things than they could.

It will remain possible, then, to think of some forms of human social organization as better than others, but not by reference to some preexisting standard. "Intellectual and moral progress is not a matter of getting closer to an antecedent goal," Rorty writes, carrying the antiteleological torch passed to him by (among others) Darwin and Kuhn, "but of surpassing the past."

Rorty suggests that our future selves, having shed the appearance-reality distinction, "would boast of being able to talk about more things" than their relatively blinkered ancestors, but this seems like a curious promise to make for an enterprise so modest as Rorty's, an enterprise devoted to seeing philosophy not as the arbiter of ultimate truths but as a set of tools to work with for human betterment. His analogies for philosophy tend to be humble, as when, in the first lecture, he insists that "rationality, thought, and cognition all began when language did," and likens human language to beaver dams: beavers build dams as the social creatures they are, humans use language as the social creatures we are. It's just what critters do, nothing more, nothing less. This aspect of Rorty's thought, his contribution to the large beaver dam known as Western philosophy, has given many people pause—not because of its claim about beavers, but because of its claim about language. *Really?* one might ask. *Our Pleistocene-era ancestors did not think until they began to talk?*

It does sound strange when you put it that way. But it speaks to something I should not leave unremarked here, and that comes up more than once in the lectures that follow. It is not only a set of propositions about language but a device for distinguishing "fantasy" from "imagination," or, as Rorty defines these terms, "novelties that do not get taken up and put to use by one's fellows and those that do." This is a critical distinction for the unfolding of human history, for "people whose novelties we cannot appropriate and utilize we call foolish, or perhaps insane. Those whose ideas strike us as useful we hail as geniuses." This is why it matters, for Rorty's argument, that one grunter of sounds can rationally assent to or criticize the sounds of a fellow grunter, and this is why Rorty wants to reserve the words "rationality," "thought," "cognition," and "language" for the process of intersubjective grunting.

At one point in the Heidegger seminar, as Rorty was proposing to us that the ironist is the person who recognizes the contingency of all languages, someone asked him why he held to such an apparently restrictive and exclusive definition of language. Don't whales and dolphins call to each other? Can't gorillas and chimpanzees learn to sign? For my part, I like to say (as I put it in *Life as Jamie Knows It*) that there has never been a discovery, in the history of human inquiries into animal cognition, that can be summed up as *Animals: Dumber than We Thought*. The findings have all run the other way, right down to tool-using octopi and crows capable of engaging in altruistic punishment. But Rorty would have none of it. Animals do what comes naturally, sure enough, but to call those activities "language," Rorty insisted, would be to head down the slippery slope on which one begins crediting the higher mammals with languages of their own and winds up with cows standing in the same direction, bees signaling the presence of pollen, and amoebas extending their pseudopods. That argument declares itself halfway through the first lecture here:

> Before there were conversational exchanges, on this view, there were neither concepts nor beliefs nor knowledge. For to say that a dog knows its master, or a baby its mother, is like saying that a lock knows when the right key has been inserted, or that a computer knows when it has been given the right password. To say that the frog's eye tells something to the frog's brain is like saying that the screwdriver tells something to the screw. The line between mechanism and something categorically distinct from mechanism comes when organisms develop social practices—uses of words—that permit those organisms to consider the relative advantages and disadvantages of alternative descriptions of things. Mechanism stops, and

freedom begins, at the point at which we can discuss which words best describe a given situation. Knowledge and freedom are coeval.

"A language is a language," I recall Rorty saying more than thirty years ago, "when you can say, in response to a word or a gesture, 'no, you don't do that in here.'" And that argument declares itself toward the end of the second lecture here:

> On [Robert] Brandom's account, to be an assertion, and so to be an example of sapience, a series of noises must be explicitly criticizable by reference to social norms. Language gets off the ground only when organisms start telling each other that they have made the wrong noise—that that is not the noise one is supposed to make in these circumstances. It gets fully under way only when the organisms are able to tell each other that they have given bad reasons for saying or doing something.

Thus, because beavers do not deliberate about better and worse ways to build dams, they are not using language in Rorty's sense, not "thinking." And, of course, every time one of us humans would grunt to Rorty, "Isn't there something wrong with thinking of thinking and language as synonyms?," Rorty would grunt back, "All right, please tell me about your extralinguistic thoughts." (He invited me to do so at some point that semester. I took the point.) There are echoes here of Wittgenstein's private language argument(s), and of Davidson's belief that a language is a language if it is translatable into *my* language. Elsewhere, Rorty makes those echoes explicit; here, Rorty's emphasis is on human agreement and disagreement, on the use of persuasion rather than force to get things done. And that emphasis is, in its turn, central to what Rorty was trying to get done.

In "Pragmatism and Romanticism," an essay published in the last year of his life (and which resonates, well beyond its title, with the third of the lectures in this volume), Rorty concludes by holding out the hope that pragmatism, like romanticism, might yet serve as a means for holding out hope—hope that we might someday come to realize that we and we alone are responsible for dreaming up new and more humane ways to live:

> If pragmatism is of any importance—if there is any difference between pragmatism and Platonism that might eventually make a difference to practice—it is not because it got something right that Platonism got wrong. It is because accepting a pragmatist outlook would change the cultural ambience for the better. It would complete the process of secularization by letting us think of the desire for non-linguistic access to the real as as hopeless as that for redemption through a beatific vision. Taking this extra step toward acknowledging our finitude would give a new resonance to Blake's dictum that "All deities reside in the human breast."

Once more with feeling, Rorty takes philosophical conflict down a notch, merely inviting us to join the pragmatist world and complete the process of secularization. But this formulation of what we will perhaps eventually have come to accept about pragmatism invites a question: How can a process of secularization be completed? Aren't we supposed to avoid thinking of human thought and human history as having an end point?

At the outset of this essay, I promised to say something about how Rorty frames his arguments in terms of what we will have appreciated about them once they have become part of ordinary human common sense. The philosopher John

Holbo once referred to this device, in a post on the academic group blog Crooked Timber, as Rorty's "rhetoric of anticipatory retrospective":

> Rorty wants to change your mind about politics. How does he do it? Not by giving you reasons not to think a certain way. Rather, by inviting you to consider the "hopeful" possibility of a future when "we" will no longer think this way. That is, he imagines a time when the sorts of people he is disagreeing with will, *ex hypothesi,* have had their paradigm shifted, so that it will simply "no longer occur to them" to think the thoughts Rorty thinks are not useful to think.

I think this is right; I read Rorty's various invocations of a "post-Philosophical society" as saying, in effect, *Come on in, the post-Philosophical water will have been fine.* But perhaps it bears noting what kind of speech act this is. Language, thought, and cognition may have begun in persuasion, in the giving of reasons, but when Rorty moves from "we should do our best to get rid" of the appearance-reality distinction to "if we did so, we should no longer wonder whether the human mind, or human language, is capable of representing reality accurately" (and the paragraph that follows), he moves from explicit persuasion to implicit invitation. It is, I think, an appropriately modest modulation.

Only once have I found that invitation unconvincing—and it involved a proposition about the present rather than a vision of the future. At the close of *Consequences of Pragmatism,* Rorty writes:

> The question of whether the pragmatist view of truth—that it is not a profitable topic—is itself true is thus a question about whether a post-Philosophical culture is a good

thing to try for. It is not a question about what the word "true" means, nor about the requirements of an adequate philosophy of language, nor about whether the world "exists independently of our minds," nor about whether the intuitions of our culture are captured in the pragmatists' slogans. There is no way in which the issue between the pragmatist and his opponent can be tightened up and resolved according to criteria agreed to by both sides. This is one of those issues which puts everything up for grabs at once—where there is no point in trying to find agreement about "the data" or about what would count as deciding the question. But the messiness of the issue is not a reason for setting it aside. The issue between religion and secularism was no less messy, but it was important that it got decided as it did.

It's the last sentence I keep stumbling on. I would like to live in a post-Philosophical culture, a secular world full of people devoted to the project of devising better and gentler ways to live; as I remark toward the end of *Life as Jamie Knows It,* I think that societies that welcome and accommodate people with disabilities are better than societies that do not. This is not the only criterion for a good society, but it is an important one, and I can believe in it and recommend it without appealing to any transcendent or transhistorical idea of truth. But I am not convinced that the issue between philosophical realists and pragmatists can be understood in terms of the issue between religion and secularism, because I am not sure that we can say that the latter issue "got decided." I wish it had, and I wish the decision had gone as Rorty claims it did, but as I write these words, I think the jury is still out, and that we still have quite a way to go if we want to take up the invitation to live in a secular world—which, apparently, many people do not want to do.

Rorty knew that he and Heidegger agreed about this much: the romantic poets did much to secularize the world—and in their better moments, they understood that they were proposing new and more humane ways of being human rather than discovering the inner human essences that had been lying buried within us all along. But Rorty himself was not a romantic poet; and though, as the lectures here demonstrate, he liked Shelley's "Defence of Poetry" for its ecumenical expansion of the word "poetry" to cover all forms of innovative thought, he would have emphatically refused the title of unacknowledged legislator. Rorty would have been satisfied, instead, with having persuaded some people, by argument and by example, that a fully secular world, in which people no longer trouble themselves about the distinction between appearance and reality, is a pleasant place to live. It is a modest goal—suitable, no doubt, to those who think modestly about things like human goals; but perhaps Rorty wanted above all, and with good reason, to teach us how to traffic in modesty.

PHILOSOPHY **as** POETRY

1

GETTING RID OF THE APPEARANCE-REALITY DISTINCTION

COMMON SENSE DISTINGUISHES BETWEEN THE APPARENT color of a thing and its real color, between the apparent motions of heavenly bodies and their real motions, between nondairy creamer and real cream, and between imitation Rolexes and real ones. But only those with a taste for philosophy ask whether real Rolexes are *really* real. Only philosophers take seriously Plato's distinction between Reality with a capital *R* and Appearance with a capital *A*. That distinction has outlived whatever usefulness it may have had. We should do our best to get rid of it.

If we did so, we should no longer wonder whether the human mind, or human language, is capable of representing reality accurately. We would stop thinking that some parts of our culture are more in touch with reality than other parts. We would express our sense of finitude not by comparing our humanity with something nonhuman but by comparing our way of being human with other, better, ways that may someday be adopted by our descendants. When we condescended to our ancestors, we would not say that they were less in touch with reality than we are, but that their imaginations were more limited than ours. We would boast of being able to talk about more things than they could.

Parmenides jump-started the Western philosophical tradition by dreaming up the notion of Reality with a capital *R*. He took the trees, the stars, the human beings, and the gods and rolled them all together into a well-rounded blob called "Being" or "the One." He then stood back from this blob and proclaimed it the only thing worth knowing about, but forever unknowable by mortals. Plato was enchanted by the notion of something even more august and unapproachable than Zeus, but he was more optimistic than Parmenides. Plato suggested that perhaps a few gifted mortals might, by replacing opinion with knowledge, gain access to what he called "the really real." Ever since Plato, there have been people who worried about whether we can gain access to Reality or whether the finitude of our cognitive faculties makes such access impossible.

Nobody, however, worries about whether we have cognitive access to trees, stars, cream, or wristwatches. We know how to tell a justified belief about such things from an unjustified one. If the word "reality" were used simply as a name for the aggregate of all such things, no problem about access to it could have arisen. The word would never have been capitalized. But when that word is given the sense that Parmenides and Plato gave it, nobody can say what would count as a justification for a belief about the thing denoted by that term. We know how to correct our beliefs about the colors of physical objects, or about the motions of planets, or the provenance of wristwatches, but we have no idea how to correct our beliefs about the ultimate nature of things. Ontology is more like a playground than like a science.

The difference between ordinary things and Reality is that when learning how to use the word "tree" we automatically acquire lots of true beliefs about trees. As Donald Davidson has argued, most of our beliefs about such things as trees and stars and wristwatches have to be true. If somebody thinks that trees are typically blue in color, and that they never grow higher than two feet, we shall conclude that whatever she may be talking about, it is not trees. There have to be many commonly accepted truths before we can raise the possibility of error. Any of these truths can be put in doubt, but not all of them at once. One can only dissent from common sense on a particular point if one is willing to accept most of the rest of what common sense says.

When it comes to Reality, however, there is no such thing as common sense. Unlike the case of trees, there are no platitudes accepted by both the vulgar and the learned. In some circles, you can get general agreement that the ultimate nature of Reality is atoms and void. In others, you can get a consensus that it is God—an immaterial, non-spatio-temporal, being. The reason quarrels among metaphysicians about the nature of Reality seem so ludicrous is that each of them feels free to pick a few of his favorite things and claim ontological privilege for them. Despite the best efforts of positivists, pragmatists, and deconstructionists, ontology is as popular among contemporary philosophers as it was in the days of Democritus and Anaxagoras. Most analytic philosophers still take the question of whether the human mind can get in touch with the really real with perfect seriousness.

My hypothesis about why ontology remains so popular is that we are still reluctant to admit that the poetic imagination sets the bounds for human thought. At the heart of philosophy's quarrel with poetry is the fear that the imagination goes all the way down—that there is nothing we talk about that we might not have talked of differently. This fear causes philosophers to become obsessed by the need to achieve *direct* access to reality. Direct, in this sense, means "unmediated by language"—for our language, we are uneasily aware, might well have been different. Before we can rid ourselves of ontology we are going to have to get rid of the idea of nonlinguistic access. This will entail getting rid of faculty psychology. We shall have to give up the picture of the human mind as divided into a good part that puts us in touch with the really real and a bad part that engages in self-stimulation and autosuggestion.

To get rid of this cluster of bad ideas we need to think of reason not as a truth-tracking faculty but as a social practice— the practice of enforcing social norms on the use of marks and noises, thereby making it possible to use words rather than blows as a way of getting things done. We need to think of imagination not as the faculty that produces visual or auditory images but as a combination of novelty and luck. To be imaginative, as opposed to being merely fantastical, is to do something new and to be lucky enough to have that novelty be adopted by one's fellow humans, incorporated into their social practices. The distinction between fantasy and imagination is between novelties that do not get taken up and put to use by one's fellows and those that do. People whose novelties we cannot appropriate and utilize we call foolish, or perhaps insane. Those whose ideas strike us as useful we hail as geniuses.

On the account of human abilities I am suggesting, the use of persuasion rather than force is an innovation comparable to the beaver's dam. Like the beavers' collaboration in getting the dam built, it is a social practice. It was initiated by the novel suggestion that we might use noises rather than physical compulsion to get other humans to cooperate with us. That suggestion gave rise to language. Rationality, thought, and cognition all began when language did. Language gets off the ground not by people giving names to things they were already thinking about but by proto-humans using noises in innovative ways, just as the proto-beavers got the practice of building dams off the ground by using sticks and mud in innovative ways. Language was, over the millennia, enlarged and rendered more flexible not by adding the names of abstract objects to those of concrete objects but by using marks and noises in ways unconnected with environmental exigencies. The distinction between the concrete and the abstract can be replaced with that between words used in making perceptual reports and those unsuitable for such use.

On the view I am sketching, expressions like "gravity" and "inalienable human rights" should not be thought of as names of entities whose nature remains mysterious but as noises and marks, the use of which by various geniuses gave rise to bigger and better social practices. Intellectual and moral progress is not a matter of getting closer to an antecedent goal but of surpassing the past. Beaver dams improved over the millennia as gifted beavers did novel things with sticks and mud, things that were then incorporated into standard dam-building practice. The arts and the sciences improved over the millennia because our more ingenious ancestors did novel things not only with seeds, clay, and metallic ores but also with noises and marks. What we call "increased knowledge" should not be thought of as increased access to the Real but as increased ability to *do* things—to take part in social practices that make possible richer and fuller human lives. This increased richness is not the effect of a magnetic attraction exerted on the human mind by the really real, nor by that mind's innate ability to penetrate the veil of appearance. It is a relation between the human present and the human past, not a relation between the human and the nonhuman.

The view that I have just finished summarizing has often been called "linguistic idealism." But that term confuses idealism, which is a metaphysical thesis about the ultimate nature of reality, with romanticism, which is a thesis about the nature of human progress. William James put the latter thesis forward in the following passage: "Mankind does nothing save through initiatives on the part of inventors, great or small, and imitations by the rest of us—these are the sole factors active in human progress. Individuals of genius show the way, and set the patterns, which common people then adopt and follow. *The rivalry of the patterns is the history of the world.*"

In that passage, James is echoing Emerson, whose essay "Circles" is perhaps the best expression of the romantic view of the nature of progress. "The life of man," Emerson writes there,

> is a self-evolving circle, which, from a ring imperceptibly small, rushes on all sides outwards to new and larger circles, and that without end. The extent to which this generation of circles, wheel without wheel, will go, depends on the force or truth of the individual soul. . . . Every ultimate fact is only the first of a new series. . . . *There is no outside, no inclosing wall, no circumference to us.* The man finishes his story—how good! how final! how it puts a new face on all things! He fills the sky. Lo! on the other side rises also a man, and draws a circle around the circle we had just pronounced the outline of the sphere. Then already is our first speaker not man, but only a first speaker. His only redress is forthwith to draw a circle outside of his antagonist. . . . In the thought of to-morrow there is a power to upheave all thy creed, all the creeds, all the literatures of the nations. . . . Men walk as prophecies of the next age. (Emphasis added)

The most important claim Emerson makes in this essay is that there is no "inclosing wall" called "the Real." There is nothing outside language to which language attempts to become adequate. Every human achievement is simply a launching pad for a greater achievement. We shall never find descriptions so perfect that imaginative redescription will become pointless. There is no destined terminus to inquiry. There are only larger human lives to be lived.

As James echoed Emerson, so Emerson was echoing the romantic poets. They too urged that men should walk as prophecies of the next age rather than in the fear of God or in the light of Reason. Shelley, in his "Defence of Poetry," deliberately and explicitly enlarged the meaning of the term "poetry." That word, he said, "may be defined to be 'the expression of the Imagination.'" In this wider sense, he said, poetry is "connate with the origin of man." It was, he went on to say, "the influence which is moved not, but moves." It is "something divine . . . at once the centre and circumference of knowledge; it is that which comprehends all science, and that to which science must be referred. It is at the same time the root and blossom of all other systems of thought." Just as the Enlightenment had deified Reason, so Shelley and other romantics deified what I have been calling "the Imagination."

It was not until Nietzsche—another disciple of Emerson's—that this romantic view of progress began to get disentangled from the claim that the intrinsic nature of reality is Spirit rather than Matter. Before Nietzsche, it was easy to conflate this central doctrine of idealist metaphysics with Emerson's profoundly antimetaphysical insistence that there is no description of things that cannot be transcended and replaced by another, more imaginative, description. But in *The Birth of Tragedy,* Nietzsche restaged the quarrel between poetry and philosophy. By treating Socrates as one more mythmaker rather than as someone who employed reason to break free of myth, he let us see Parmenides and Plato as all-too-strong poets. His way of looking at the philosophical tradition these men initiated made it possible to see both German idealism and British empiricism as outgrowths of the urge to find unmediated access to the real. Both movements were hoping to find something unredescribable, something that would trump poetry. Nietzsche helped us think of Kant and John Stuart Mill as two of a kind: both were anxious to find an "inclosing wall," one that the imagination could not leap across.

In his later work, Nietzsche echoed Schiller and Shelley when he urged us to become "the poets of our own lives" (*die Dichter unseres Lebens*). But he wanted to go further. He said over and over again that not just human lives but the world in which those lives are lived is a creation of the human imagination. In *The Gay Science* he summarized his criticism of Socrates and Plato in the following passage:

> [The higher human being deludes himself]: he calls his nature contemplative and thereby overlooks the fact that he is also the actual poet and ongoing author of life [*der eigentlich Dichter und Fortdichter des Lebens*]. . . . It is we, the thinking-sensing ones [*die Denkend-Empfindenden*], who really and continually make something that is not yet there: the whole perpetually growing world of valuations, colours, weights, perspectives, scales, affirmations, and negations. This poem that we have invented is constantly internalized, drilled, translated into flesh and reality, indeed, into the commonplace, by the so-called practical human beings (our actors). Only we have created the world that concerns human beings!

A conservative interpretation of this passage would treat it as saying that although of course nature is not made by us, it has no significance for us until we have topped it up. We overlay nature with another world, the world that concerns us, the only world in which a properly human life can be led. The senses give both us and the animals access to the natural world, but we humans have superimposed a second world by internalizing a poem, thereby making the two worlds seem equally inescapable. Outside of the natural sciences, reason works within the second world, following paths that the imagination has cleared. But inside those sciences, nature itself shows the way.

That conservative interpretation might have satisfied the romantic poets. It would have provided a plausible gloss on Shelley's claim that the poets are the unacknowledged legislators of the world. It is consistent with the view of the relation between the cognitive, the moral, and the aesthetic that Schiller offered in *Letters on the Aesthetic Education of Man*. Nevertheless, that interpretation is insufficiently radical. It does not take account of Nietzsche's frequent polemics against the appearance-reality distinction—against the idea that there *is* a way that nature is in itself, apart from human needs and interests

He says in the *Nachlass*, for example, that "the dogmatic idea of 'things that have a constitution in themselves' is one with which one must break absolutely." He spells out his point by saying: "That things possess a constitution in themselves quite apart from interpretation and subjectivity, is a quite idle hypothesis; it presupposes that interpretation and subjectivity are not essential, that a thing freed from all relationships would still be a thing."

In passages such as this one Nietzsche brushes aside the common-sense claim that there is a way Reality is independent of the way human beings describe it. He was equally contemptuous of the more sophisticated Kantian idea that an unknowable non-spatio-temporal thing-in-itself lurks behind the phenomenal world. Nietzsche's teaching does, however, bear some resemblance to Hegel's claim that Nature is but a moment in the developing self-consciousness of Spirit. Nietzsche would certainly second Hegel's insistence that we not conceive of knowledge as a medium for getting in touch with Reality but instead think of it as a way in which Spirit enlarges itself. But Nietzsche differs from Hegel in rejecting the idea of a natural terminus to the progress of this self-consciousness—a final unity in which all tensions are resolved, in which appearance is put behind us and true reality revealed. Unlike Hegel, and like Emerson, Nietzsche is making a purely negative point. He is not saying that Spirit alone is really real, but that we should stop asking what is really real.

Nietzsche never developed this view in any detail, nor did he succeed in making it perspicuous. It is, as many commentators have pointed out, impossible to reconcile with many other things that he said. It is incompatible, in particular, with his repeated claim that he himself is the first philosopher to be free from illusion. The only criticism of his predecessors to which Nietzsche is entitled is that they were all too timid to break out of the Platonic account of the human situation, too hesitant to sketch a larger circle than the one Plato had drawn. Nor can Nietzsche's prophecy of a postmetaphysical age be squared with the passages in the later writings in which Nietzsche seems to be claiming that the will to power is the only thing that is really real. Those are the passages that Heidegger seized upon in order to caricature Nietzsche as "the last metaphysician," the proponent of an inverted Platonism.

Despite Nietzsche's own inconsistencies, the romantic anti-Platonism he put forward in the passages I have quoted is a coherent philosophical position. It can be buttressed and clarified by bringing Nietzsche together with the work of various twentieth-century analytic philosophers. In what follows, I shall be rehearsing some arguments put forward by

Wittgenstein, and some others developed by Wilfrid Sellars, Donald Davidson, and Robert Brandom. I think that these arguments help give a plausible sense both to the claim that nature itself is a poem that we humans have written and to the claim that the imagination is the principle vehicle of human progress.

The analytic philosophers I have listed are united in their repudiation of empiricism. They debunk the idea that animals and human beings take in information about the world through their sense organs. They undermine the idea that the senses provide an unchanging and solid core around which the imagination weaves wispy and ephemeral circles. On their account, the senses do not enjoy a special relation to reality that distinguishes their deliverances from those of the imagination.

The idea of such a privileged relation goes back to Plato's analogy between the mind and a wax tablet, and to Aristotle's suggestion that the sensory organs take on the qualities of the sensed object. Plato, Aristotle, and contemporary cognitive scientists all describe sense perception as a way of getting something that is outside the organism inside the organism— either by way of identity, as in Aristotle, or by way of representation, as in Lockean empiricism and contemporary cognitive science. On this traditional account, there is a big difference between a mechanism like a thermostat that simply responds to changes in the environment and an organism with a nervous system capable of containing representations of the environment. The thermostat just reacts. The organism acquires information.

On the antiempiricist view, a view Nietzsche would have welcomed had he encountered it, there is no difference between the thermostat, the dog, and the prelinguistic infant other than differing levels of complexity of reaction to environmental stimuli. The brutes and the infants are capable of discriminative responses, but not of acquiring information. For there is no such thing as the acquisition of information until there is language in which to formulate that information. Information came into the universe when the first hominids began to justify their actions to one another by making assertions and backing those assertions up with further assertions. Before the practice of giving and asking for reasons developed, the noises these hominids made to each other did not convey information in any more interesting sense than that in which the motion of ambient molecules conveys information to the thermostat, or the digestive enzymes convey information to the contents of the stomach.

To accept this alternative account of sense perception means abandoning the traditional story about language learning—one in which language got its start by people giving names to what they were already thinking about. For on this account all awareness that is more than the ability to respond differentially to varied stimuli is, as Sellars said, "a linguistic affair." The brutes, the sunflowers, the thermostats, and the human infants can produce differential responses, but awareness, information, and knowledge are possible only after the acquisition of language.

On the view common to Sellars and Wittgenstein, to possess a concept is to be familiar with the use of a linguistic expression. Whereas empiricists think of concepts as mental representations, Sellars and Wittgenstein have no use for what Willard Van Orman Quine called "the idea idea." Philosophers who still adhere to this idea are forced to take on the well-nigh-impossible burden of explaining the relations between neural process and the various representations that make up this realm. Abandoning the idea idea means treating the possession of a mind as the possession of certain social skills—the skills required to give and ask for reasons. To have a mind is not to have a movie theater inside the skull, with successive representations of the surroundings flashing on the screen. It is the ability to use persuasion to get what one wants.

Before there were conversational exchanges, on this view, there were neither concepts nor beliefs nor knowledge. For to say that a dog knows its master, or a baby its mother, is like saying that a lock knows when the right key has been inserted, or that a computer knows when it has been given the right password. To say that the frog's eye tells something to the frog's brain is like saying that the screwdriver tells something to the screw. The line between mechanism and something categorically distinct from mechanism comes when organisms develop social practices—uses of words—that permit those organisms to consider the relative advantages and disadvantages of alternative descriptions of things. Mechanism stops, and freedom begins, at the point at which we can discuss which words best describe a given situation. Knowledge and freedom are coeval.

On the romantic view I am commending, the imagination is the source of freedom because it is the source of language. It is, as Shelley put it, root as well as blossom. It is not that we first spoke a language that simply reported what was going on around us and later enlarged this language by imaginative redescription. Rather, imaginativeness goes all the way down. The concepts of redness and roundness are as much imaginative creations as those of God, of the positron, and of constitutional democracy. Getting the word "red" into circulation was a feat on a par with Newton's persuading people to use the term "gravity." For nobody knew what redness was before some early hominids began talking about the differences in the colors of things, just as nobody knew what gravity was before Newton began describing an occult force responsible for both ballistic trajectories and planetary orbits. It took imaginative genius to suggest that everybody make the same noise at the sight of blood, of maple leaves in autumn, and of the western sky at sunset. It was only when such suggestions were taken seriously and put into practice that hominids began to have minds.

As for the concept "round," it was not obvious that the full moon and the trunks of trees had anything in common before some genius began to use a noise that we would translate as "round." Nothing at all was obvious, because obviousness is not a notion that can be applied to organisms that do not use language. The thermostats, the brutes, and the prelinguistic human infants do not find anything obvious, even though they all respond to stimuli in predictable ways. The notion of prelinguistic obviousness is inseparable from the Cartesian story about the spectator sitting in a little theater inside the skull, watching representations come and go, giving them names as they pass. Sellars parodied that account when he described a child mind confronting the manifold of sense. "Ah," this mind says to itself, "there it is now! And another one! And another—a splendid specimen! By the methods of Mill, *this* must be what Mother calls 'red'!"

In the Cartesian picture, the child mind already knows the difference between colors and shapes, and between red and blue, before having learned any words. The contrasting view is suggested by Nietzsche in another passage from the *Nachlass.* There he writes, "In a world in which there is no being, a certain calculable world of identical cases must first be created." He would done better to have written, "in a world in which there is no knowledge" rather than, "in a world in which there is no being." If we rewrite in that way, we can read him as saying that you cannot have knowledge without identifiable things, and that there is no such thing as identification until people can use terms such as "same shape" and "different color." We begin to have knowledge only when we can formulate such thoughts as that this thing has a different color than that but the same shape. The empiricist tradition attributes the ability to have this thought to brutes and pre-linguistic infants. The antiempiricist view I am offering says that there is no more reason to attribute it to them than to attribute the thought "It is cooler than it used to be" to a thermostat.

Imagination, in the sense in which I am using the term, is not a distinctively human capacity. It is, as I said earlier, the ability to come up with socially useful novelties. This is an ability Newton shared with certain eager and ingenious beavers. But giving and asking for reasons *is* distinctively human, and is coextensive with rationality. The more an organism can get what it wants by persuasion rather than force, the more rational it is. Ulysses, for example, was more rational than Achilles. But you cannot use persuasion if you cannot talk. No imagination, no language. No linguistic change, no moral or intellectual progress. Rationality is a matter of making allowed moves within language games. Imagination creates the games that reason proceeds to play. Then, exemplified by people such as Plato and Newton, it keeps modifying those games so that playing them is more interesting and profitable. Reason cannot get outside the latest circle that imagination has drawn. It is in this sense, and only in this sense, that imagination holds the primacy.

The Nietzschean view I have been sketching is often described as the doctrine that everything is "constituted" by language, or that everything is "socially constructed," or that everything is "mind dependent." But these descriptions are hopelessly misleading. Words like "constitution" and "construction" and "dependence," in the language games that are their original homes, refer to causal relations. They are invoked to explain how something came into existence or can continue to exist. We say, for example, that the United States of America was constituted out of the thirteen original colonies, that wooden houses are constructed by carpenters, and that children depend on their parents for their support.

But philosophers who say, misleadingly, that redness, like gravity, is constituted by language, or that roundness, like gender, is a social construction, do not mean to suggest that one sort of entity was brought into existence by another sort. They are not offering a hypothesis about causal relations—a hypothesis that is obviously absurd. Causal relations hold only within what Nietzsche called "a certain calculable world of identical cases"—a world of identifiable objects. We can investigate causal relations once we have identified such objects, but there is no point in asking where the world that contains such objects comes from. You can ask sensible paleontological questions about where trees and beavers came from, and sensible astrophysical questions about where stars came from, but you cannot give a sense to the question of where spatio-temporal objects in general came from.

Kant, unfortunately, did pose that bad question. He then told an imaginative story about how the thing-in-itself gets whipped into spatio-temporal shape by the transcendental ego. The blatant internal incoherence of that story soon gave idealism a bad name. But the Nietzschean view I have been outlining avoids any such story, and nevertheless preserves what was true in idealism—namely, the thesis that there is no such thing as preconceptual cognitive access to objects. Our only cognitive access to beavers, trees, and stars consists in our ability to use the words "beaver," "tree," and "star."

Kant's mistake was to formulate a thesis about the inseparability of identifiable things from our thoughts about them as a thesis about where those things came from. Hegel, by substituting absolute for transcendental idealism, avoided this mistake. But Hegel phrased his doctrines in terms of the Platonic-Cartesian distinction between material and immaterial being, and he was inspired by the hope of transcending the finite human condition. So Hegelianism succumbed to positivistic criticism. The historicism that Hegel took from Herder had to be reformulated by post-Nietzschean philosophers such as Heidegger before it could be disentangled from Hegel's awkward attempts at eschatology.

Defenders of the Platonic tradition often criticize views of the sort I am putting forward by interpreting them as claiming that nothing was red or round before the first hominids began to converse, and that mountains came into existence only when they began to use a noise meaning "mountain." But this is a caricature. Wittgenstein's point is not about when things came into existence but about how language and thought did. It is rather that, as he put it, naming requires a lot of stage setting in the language: it is no use pointing to a red and round ball, uttering "red," and expecting the baby to grasp that you are directing its attention to a color rather than to a shape. Wittgenstein seems to have been the first to remark that the empiricist picture of language learning requires us to think of babies as talking to themselves in Mentalese, the language that Sellars's child was speaking when it figured out that this was what Mother calls "red."

The issue about prelinguistic awareness that pits Wittgenstein, Sellars, Davidson, and Brandom against Jerry Fodor and other fans of cognitive science may seem remote from the question of the priority of the imagination. But I have been trying to persuade you that that issue is decisive for the question of whether Nietzsche was right to think of the world as our poem rather than as something that somehow communicates information about itself to us. How we answer that question determines whether we think of the progress human beings have made in the last few millennia as a matter of expanding our imaginations or as an increased ability to represent reality accurately.

When Nietzsche urged us to "see science through the optic of art," he was suggesting that we should see new scientific theories not as representations of the real but as poetic achievements. Shelley's dictum that the poets are the unacknowledged legislators of the world, interpreted along Nietzschean lines, is the claim that Newton was to the laws of motion as Solon was to the laws of Athens. Both men made imaginative proposals about what language should be used to achieve a given purpose. In Solon's case this purpose was to achieve greater social order in his city. In Newton's case it was to render physical phenomena more predictable. Both sets of proposals, for a time at least, served those purposes well. The question of whether either or both got reality right need not arise.

This view of science is anathema to philosophers whose favorite things are elementary physical particles. These philosophers conflate the question "Have we, in recent centuries, learned more about how things work?" with the quite different question "Have we learned more about what is really real?" The answer to the first question is obviously "yes." The answer to the second will be "yes" only if we assume that finding out how things work is a matter of finding a description of them as they really are. It is just that assumption that both the German idealists and Nietzsche challenged. But whereas the idealists thought that philosophy could answer questions about the nature of Reality that empirical science could not, Nietzsche just wanted to stop people from posing such questions.

Nietzsche thought that Plato's success in putting the term "really real" into circulation was a great imaginative achievement. But the answer to a great poem is a still better poem, and that is what Nietzsche thought of himself as writing. He asked us to see, as he put it in *The Twilight of the Idols,* that "the true world" is a fable, a myth concocted by Parmenides and Plato. The problem, he said, is not that it is a fable, but that it is a fable that has by now exhausted its utility. We should not say that the hope of knowing the intrinsic nature of Reality was an illusion, because, as Nietzsche rightly says, when we give up the notion of a true world, we give up that of an illusory world as well. The difference between a good old poem and new better poem is not the difference between a bad representation of Reality and a better one.

In this lecture, I have been trying to persuade you that Nietzsche wrote the better poem. As I see it, the romantic movement marked the beginning of the attempt to replace the tale told by the Greek philosophers with a better tale. The old story was about how human beings might manage to get back in touch with something from which they had somehow become estranged—something that is not itself a human creation but stands over and against all such creations. The new story is about how human beings continually strive to overcome the human past in order to create a better human future.

To convince you that the new story is better for our purposes than the old, I have been asking you to think of what we often call the "beginnings of scientific rationality" in ancient Greece in the context of "the quarrel between poetry and philosophy." To take the side of the poets in this quarrel is to say that there are many descriptions of the same things and events, and that there is no neutral standpoint from which to judge the superiority of one description over another. Philosophy stands in opposition to poetry just insofar as it insists that there is such a standpoint.

Plato said that we should try to substitute logic for rhetoric, the application of criteria for imaginative power. By tracing an argumentative path back to first principles, Plato thought, we can attain the goal that he described as "reaching a place beyond hypotheses." When we have reached that goal, we shall be immune to the seductive effects of redescription, for we shall have established the sort of "ostensive tie" between ourselves and the really real that, on the empiricist view, visual perception establishes with colors and shapes. Just as we cannot deny the evidence of our senses—cannot make ourselves believe that something is blue when our eyes tell us that it is red—so the Platonic philosopher cannot make himself doubt what he sees when he reaches the top of Plato's divided line. But for the poets, logical argumentation—conformity to the rules of deductive validity—is just one rhetorical technique among others. Nietzsche and Wittgenstein both suggest substituting Emerson's metaphor of endlessly expanding circles for Plato's metaphor of ascent to the indubitable.

When he used the figure of the divided line to symbolize the ascent from opinion to knowledge, and when he used the allegory of the cave for the same purpose, Plato was implicitly recognizing that the only way to escape redescription was to attain a kind of knowledge that was not discursive—a kind that did not rely on choice of a particular linguistic formulation. To reach truth that one cannot be argued out of is to escape from the linguistically expressible to the ineffable. Only the ineffable—what is not describable at all—cannot be described differently.

When Nietzsche says that a thing conceived apart from its relationships would not be a thing, he should be read as saying that since all language is a matter of relating some things to other things, the unrelatable is necessarily ineffable and unknowable. Language establishes relationships by tying blood in with sunsets and full moons with tree trunks. Lack of describability means lack of relations, so our only access to the indescribable must be the sort of direct awareness that the empiricist has to redness and that the mystic has to God. Much of the history of Western philosophy, from Plotinus and Meister Eckhart down to Hume and Russell, is the history of the quest for such direct awareness.

I have been arguing in this lecture that the quarrel between the later Wittgenstein and traditional British empiricism epitomizes the quarrel that philosophy has had with poetry, and that the analytic philosophers who have lined up on Wittgenstein's side have provided valuable support to Emerson's romantic account of progress in terms of ever-expanding circles. In my next lecture, I shall offer an account of non-Wittgensteinian analytic philosophy as an attempt to retain the Platonic story about progress and to maintain, against Emerson, that there really is an "inclosing wall," a circumference to human existence—that philosophy can describe the unchanging framework within which dramas of history are enacted. In the third and final lecture, I shall return to the topic of romanticism. There I shall argue that admirers of Shelley and Emerson should beware of the temptation to turn the poetic imagination into a means of direct access to reality—the temptation to model the imagination as a truth-tracking faculty. The moral of the lectures taken together is that philosophy and poetry can coexist peaceably if both sides are willing to give up on the attempt to transcend human finitude.

2

UNIVERSALIST GRANDEUR AND ANALYTIC PHILOSOPHY

PHILOSOPHY OCCUPIES AN IMPORTANT PLACE IN CULTURE only when things seem to be falling apart—when cherished beliefs are threatened. At such times, intellectuals start to prophesy a new age. They reinterpret the past by reference to an imagined future, and offer suggestions about what should be preserved and what must be discarded. Those whose suggestions prove most influential win a place on the list of "great philosophers."

For example, when prayer and priestcraft began to be viewed with suspicion, Plato and Aristotle suggested ways in which we might hold on to the idea that human beings, unlike the beasts that perish, have a special relation to the ruling powers of the universe. When Copernicus and Galileo erased the world picture that had comforted Aquinas and Dante, Spinoza and Kant taught Europe how to replace love of God with love of Truth, and how to replace obedience to the divine will with moral purity. When the democratic revolutions and industrialization forced us to rethink the nature of the social bond, Marx and Mill stepped forward with some useful suggestions.

In the course of the twentieth century, there were no crises of the sort that set the agenda for Western intellectuals between 1600 and 1900. There was no intellectual struggle comparable in scale to the warfare between science and theology. As high culture became more thoroughly secularized, the educated classes of Europe and the Americas became complacently materialist in their understanding of how the universe works. They also become complacently utilitarian and experimentalist in their evaluations of proposed social and political initiatives. They came to share the same utopian vision of a global commonwealth in which human rights are respected, equality of opportunity assured, and the chances of human happiness thereby increased. Nowadays, serious political argument is about how this goal might be reached, not about whether that goal is the correct one to pursue.

That is why the controversies between Russell and Bergson, or Heidegger and Cassirer, or the young Wittgenstein and his older self, or Carnap and Quine, or Ayer and Austin, or Fodor and Davidson, or Habermas and Gadamer, had little resonance outside the borders of philosophy departments. Philosophers' explanations of how objects make sentences true, or of how the mind is related to the brain, or of how free will and mechanism might be reconciled, do not intrigue most contemporary intellectuals. Such problems, preserved in amber as textbook "problems of philosophy," still capture the imagination of bright students. But no one would claim that discussion of them is central to intellectual life. Solving those very problems was all-important for contemporaries of Spinoza, but when contemporary philosophers insist that they are "fundamental" or "perennial," nobody takes their claims seriously.

Nevertheless, the quarrel between philosophy and poetry that I sketched yesterday, the one that was revitalized by the romantic movement, still goes on. Nowadays it takes the form of a face-off between philosophers described (though not by themselves) as "postmodern relativists" and their opponents. The two camps disagree about whether Plato was right that humans beings can transcend their finitude by searching for truth or whether Nietzsche was right to treat both Platonism and religion as escapist fantasies. Philosophers who view postmodernism with alarm typically argue that Nietzsche was right about religion but wrong about Platonism. They resist the Nietzschean idea that reason works only within the limits that imagination has set—that rationality is simply a matter of making acceptable moves within a set of social practices. They agree with Plato that there is more to reason than that, and they regard their own discipline as a paradigm of rationality.

In this lecture, I shall first describe how the current version of the Plato-Nietzsche opposition looks when it is seen as the issue between analytic and nonanalytic philosophy. Then I shall redescribe it, this time as a disagreement between two groups of analytic philosophers: the ones whom I heroized in my first lecture—Wittgenstein, Sellars, Davidson, and Brandom—and their opponents. The latter resist the "social practice" account of mind and language, in part because they see it as lending aid and comfort to postmodernist relativism.

An account of what is going on these days in the world's philosophy departments must start by distinguishing between social and political philosophy on the one hand and the so-called core areas of philosophy on the other. The latter areas include metaphysics, epistemology, philosophy of mind, and philosophy of language. The philosophers who work at the margins usually have little communication with those at the core. Those who specialize in social and political theory typically read many more books by professors of political science or law than books written by fellow philosophers. They do not read books about the relation between the mind and the body, or that between language and reality. The converse also holds. The authors of books on the latter topics are typically ill informed about the state of sociopolitical theory. That these two sorts of specialists are members of the same academic department is an accident of university history.

The difference between these two broad areas of interest is highlighted by the fact that the split between "analytic" philosophy and "nonanalytic" philosophy (the kind of philosophy sometimes called "Continental") has little relevance to books that touch on political issues. Neither label can usefully be applied to such figures as Jürgen Habermas, Nancy Fraser, Joseph Raz, and Pierre Manent. These philosophers are concerned with the same issues as are nonphilosophers such as Michael Walzer, Ronald Dworkin, Richard Posner, and Ulrich Beck—questions about how we might change our social and political institutions so as better to combine freedom with order and justice.

Once we bracket off social and political philosophy, however, the analytic versus Continental split becomes the most salient feature of the contemporary philosophical scene. Most analytic philosophers would still agree with Frank Ramsey that Bertrand Russell's theory of descriptions is a paradigm of philosophy. Most nonanalytic philosophers think that nothing Russell did compares in importance with Hegel's *The Phenomenology of Spirit* or with Heidegger's *Letter on Humanism*.

Someone who thinks of herself as an analytic philosopher of mind and language will almost certainly be familiar with Russell's theory. But she may never have read, and may have little ambition to read, either Hegel or Heidegger. Yet if you teach philosophy in most nonanglophone countries, you must be prepared to talk about both *The Phenomenology of Spirit* and *Letter on Humanism*. You can, however, skip the theory of descriptions. Most Brazilian, Turkish, and Polish philosophers, for example, manage to get by with only a vague idea of why their anglophone colleagues believe Russell to have been an important figure. Conversely, most Australian and US philosophers are puzzled that in much of the world the study of Hegel is still thought essential to a sound training in their discipline.

In order to bring out the contrast between the self-images of these two kinds of philosophers, let me briefly describe the theory of descriptions. Russell designed it to answer such questions as "Given that the words used to form the subjects of sentences refer to things, and that a sentence is true if things are as the sentence says they are, how is it that some true sentences containing a referring expression become false if one substitutes another expression that refers to the same thing?" Russell's example of two such sentences was "George IV wished to know whether Scott was the author of *Waverly*," which is true, and "George IV wished to know whether Scott was Scott," which is false.

The theory of descriptions answers this question by saying that the description "the author of *Waverly*," unlike the word "Scott," does not pick out a particular individual. What George IV really wanted to know, Russell said, was whether there existed an individual who had the property of being the author of *Waverly* and who was identical with Scott. Putting the matter that way, he claimed, reveals the true "logical form" of the sentence in question and solves the puzzle.

That it has this logical form can be revealed, Russell said, by invoking distinctions that were built into the new symbolic logic developed by Russell's master, Gottlob Frege. A knowledge of this logic is still regarded by most anglophone philosophers as essential to philosophical competence. Many of their nonanglophone colleagues find it optional.

If you suspect that Russell's theory provides a clever answer to a pointless question, you are in good company. You have many eminent contemporary philosophers on your side. These philosophers, ranging from the Heideggerians to the Davidsonians, do not think that questions about how things in the world make sentences true are of any interest. They take these questions to be good examples of what Berkeley described as kicking up the dust and then complaining that one cannot see. The dust cloud is created, on their view, by taking seriously the Platonic idea that some ways of speaking are better suited to put us in touch with the really real than others.

Philosophers who prefer Russell to Hegel and Heidegger often point out that the tradition in philosophy that Frege and Russell founded makes a virtue of spelling out exactly what questions it is currently attempting to answer. Whether or not you find the analytic philosophers' problems intriguing, at least you know what they are. The only question is whether you should bother about them. Analytic philosophers typically claim that the issues they discuss should intrigue you because certain intuitions that you yourself had before you ever opened a philosophy book are in tension with one another. One such intuition is that sentences are made true by the extralinguistic entities that they are about. The value of the theory of descriptions is that it rescues this intuition from some apparent counterexamples.

Hegel and Heidegger, by contrast, did not care much about either common sense or ordinary language. Whereas Frege and Russell hoped to make things clearer, Hegel and Heidegger hoped to make things different. Russell's admirers want to get things straight by finding perspicuous relations between your previously existing intuitions. Hegel, Heidegger, and their admirers hope to change not only your intuitions but your sense of who you are, and your notion of what it is most important to think about. To use Emerson's language, they are trying to draw a larger circle—trying to lure their readers out into as yet uncharted spaces. In those spaces, old intuitions are up for grabs, and it is hard to argue in a straight line. It is hard to know when one has got something right, because it is never quite clear what exactly one is talking about.

In the hope of getting you to change your self-image, your priorities, and your intuitions, Hegel tells you that the Absolute alone is true and Heidegger that language is the house of Being. If you stop at each such sentence and pause to ask yourself whether it has been backed up with a sound argument, you will never finish their books. To get through their books, you must temporarily suspend disbelief, get into the swing of the story that is being told, pick up the jargon as you go along, and then decide, after having given the entire book the most sympathetic reading you can, whether to move out into uncharted space.

If you lay down those books feeling no temptation to make any such move, you may conclude that Hegel and Heidegger are, at best, failed poets and, at worst, self-infatuated obscurantists. If this is your reaction, you will be in good company. You will have many eminent contemporary philosophers on your side. A willingness to define one's terms, list one's premises, and argue in a straight line is regarded by most admirers of Russell as essential to doing good philosophy. For admirers of Hegel and Heidegger, however, requests for definitions and premises are symptoms of unwillingness to let philosophy attempt its transformative task.

Given all these differences between analytic and nonanalytic philosophy, one might wonder whether there is any point in treating Frege, Russell, Hegel, and Heidegger as in the same line of business. The two sorts of philosophers have, in fact, often tried to excommunicate each other. Analytic philosophers often describe Hegel and Heidegger as "not really doing philosophy." Hegelians and Heideggerians typically rejoin that their analytic colleagues are intellectual cowards who feel insecure outside a familiar professional environment. This exchange of insults has been going on for some fifty years and seems unlikely to cease.

My own view is that all four of the thinkers I have just mentioned are usefully grouped together. This is because they were all trying to answer questions first formulated explicitly by Plato: What makes human beings special? What do we have that the other animals lack? What self-image will do proper justice to our uniqueness?

Plato's response was that we are special because we, unlike the animals, can know how things, including ourselves, really are. He urged that our self-image should be that of beings capable of grasping universal and unconditional truth—truth that is a product neither of imaginative redescription nor of contingent circumstance. Frege and Russell thought that Plato's answer was roughly right. They saw their own work as helping us answer a question Plato had tried to answer— namely, what is the relation between our beliefs and reality such that we can have at least some of the knowledge we claim to have?

Earlier answers to that question were inadequate, Frege and Russell thought, because philosophers from Plato to Kant had failed to zero in on language as the medium in which human beings represent reality to themselves and therefore had not reflected sufficiently on the nature of linguistic representations. So they had not paid proper attention to logical form, nor to the puzzles to which Russell's theory of descriptions offered solutions. Russell's admirers say that you will not think discussion of the relation between George IV and Scott pointless once you realize that solving such puzzles is essential to understanding the relation between language and the world, and thus to understanding the nature of truth.

As I said in my first lecture, Nietzsche gave a different answer than Plato's to the question about what makes human beings special. He said it was our ability to transform ourselves into something new, rather than our ability to know what we ourselves really are or what the universe is really like. He mocked Plato's appearance-reality distinction, a distinction that most analytic philosophers still take for granted.

Most contemporary philosophers who take Hegel and Heidegger seriously share Nietzsche's doubts about the utility of that distinction. They usually try to replace it with the distinction between the past and the present—between earlier and later stages of the world spirit's progress. Such philosophers read both Hegel and the romantic poets as precursors of Nietzsche's revolt against Platonism. Hegel's story about how human beings have drawn successively wider circles around themselves prepares the way for Nietzsche's claim that the point of being human is to achieve self-creation through self-redescription.

Those who read Hegel in this way typically go on to read Heidegger as the first thinker to have tried to mediate the conflict between Plato's and Nietzsche's suggestions about what makes human beings special. So read, Heidegger's later writings tell a story about how Western intellectuals started off striving to gain self-knowledge but eventually decided to settle for self-creation. Like Hegel's, Heidegger's narrative of maturation is not an attempt to say something about human beings in general, but rather to exhibit the difference between the Western past and the Western present. Telling stories of this sort has nothing to do with answering the questions about the scope and limits of human knowledge that were raised by Hume and Kant, nor with those about how things make sentences true that were asked by Frege and Russell.

Philosophers in the Hegel-Nietzsche-Heidegger tradition are suspicious of what I shall call "universalistic grandeur"— the sort of grandeur that is achieved in mathematics and in mathematical physics. Both numbers and elementary particles display the imperturbability and invulnerability traditionally attributed to the divine. The study of both produces structures of great beauty. The same impulse that led Plato to think that what he called "the really real" must be more like a number than like a lump of dirt leads many recent analytic philosophers both to take modern physical science as the overarching framework within which philosophical inquiry is to be conducted and to try to make philosophy itself into a science. They think that physics not only tells you how things work but also tells you what is really real. So they think it important to develop a naturalized epistemology and a naturalized semantics, in order to fit mind and language into a physicalistic world picture.

That is why many analytic philosophers think of the struggle they are waging against those whom they describe as "relativists" or "irrationalists" or "deniers of truth" as a defense of science against its enemies. Many of them think of science as pre-Galilean intellectuals thought of religion—as the place where the human mind comes up against something of transcendent significance. They think of physical science both as grasping the intrinsic nature of the really real and as the paradigmatically human activity. They regard refusal to grant science this exalted status as a symptom of spiritual degradation. Thus Russell, at the beginning of the last century, reacted against the line of thought that William James called "pragmatism" and his Oxford friend F. C. S. Schiller called "humanism" by writing as follows:

Greatness of soul is not fostered by those philosophies
which assimilate the universe to Man. Knowledge is a form
of union of Self and not-Self; like all union, it is impaired
by domination, and therefore by any attempt to force the
universe into conformity with what we find in ourselves.
There is a widespread philosophical tendency towards the
view which tells us that Man is the measure of all things,
that truth is man-made. . . . This view . . . is untrue; but in
addition to being untrue, it has the effect of robbing phil-
osophic contemplation of all that gives it value. . . . The
free intellect will see as God might see, without a here and
now, without hopes and fears . . . calmly, dispassionately,
in the sole and exclusive desire of knowledge—knowledge
as impersonal, as purely contemplative, as it is possible for
man to attain.

Thomas Nagel, a contemporary critic of postmodern relativism, shares Russell's contempt for those who believe that,
as James put it, "the trail of the human serpent is over all."
He describes what he calls "the outermost framework of all
thoughts" as "a conception of what is objectively the case—
what is the case without subjective or relative qualification."
In response to pragmatists and historicists who reject the idea
of an outermost framework and argue that all justification is
by the lights of a particular time and place, Nagel says,

Claims to the effect that a type of judgment expresses a
local point of view are inherently objective in intent. They
suggest a picture of the true sources of those judgments
that places them in an unconditional context. The judgment of relativity or conditionality cannot be applied to
the judgment of relativity itself. . . . There may be some
subjectivists, perhaps calling themselves pragmatists, who
present subjectivism as applying even to itself. But then

what they say does not call for a reply, since it is just a report of what the subjectivist finds it agreeable to say.

Russell and Nagel share Plato's aspiration to universalist grandeur. Both agree with him that there is, in the end, no middle way between making unconditional truth-claims and simply saying whatever strikes you as agreeable to say. There is nothing in between the attempt to attain the universal, the aspiration that sets humans apart from the brutes, and giving way to our lower desires, our transitory feelings, and our unjustifiable idiosyncrasies. So the pragmatists' suggestion that contemporary physical science be thought of simply as the best way to cope with our environment that we have come up with so far strikes Russell and Nagel as a symptom of moral weakness as well as of intellectual error. So does Emerson's suggestion that there is no "inclosing wall," no permanent circumference to human life—only endless opportunities to transform ourselves by expanding our imaginations.

So much for the split between analytic and nonanalytic philosophy. Now I want to turn to the debate going on within analytic philosophy between Wittgensteinian "social practice" theorists and those philosophers who look to cognitive science for an understanding of how mind and language work. The Wittgensteinians think it a mistake to treat mind and language as entities that have either elementary parts or a structure or inner workings. They do not believe that there are things called "beliefs" or "meanings" into which minds and languages can usefully be broken up. They think that the cognitive scientists fail to understand that mind, like language, is a social phenomenon, not something located between the ears.

Both sides agree that what makes human beings special is their possession of mind and language. They also agree that we should talk about mind and language in a way that is consistent with modern science—that is, without appealing to the nonphysical entities postulated by Plato, Augustine, and Descartes. But there the similarities end. One side wants to get psychology in touch with neurology in roughly the same way that chemistry was brought together with physics and biology. Such philosophers find it useful and important to say that the mind is, in some important sense, the brain. So they spend much of their time analyzing concepts like "belief" and "meaning" in order to show how beliefs and meanings can reside within the collection of physical particles that is the human central nervous system.

The Wittgensteinians, by contrast, think that identifying the mind with the brain is thoroughly misleading. As they see it, cognitive scientists are taking for granted that what worked for matter—namely, explaining macrostructural behavior by specifying transactions between microstructural components—will also work for mind. These philosophers agree that there is much to be discovered about how the brain works, but they doubt that even an ideal neurophysiology would tell us anything interesting about mind or language. For, they insist, the mind is no more the brain than the computer is the hardware. Mind and brain, culture and biology, swing as free from one another as do silicon chips and programs. They can and should be studied independently.

Understanding mind and language, the Wittgensteinians say, is a matter of understanding culture, and, in particular, understanding the evolution of the social practices in which we presently engage. Cultural evolution, to be sure, could not have begun until biological evolution had reached a certain point. But explanations of human behavior that tie in with neurology and with evolutionary biology will tell us, at most, about what we share with the chimpanzees. We can learn about the processes that mediated between those ancestors and ourselves only by constructing a narrative, telling a story about how their social practices gradually mutated into ours.

These "social practice" theorists think that the best way to show that we need not postulate immaterial entities to explain our uniqueness is to tell a story about how animal grunts mutated into human assertions. On Brandom's account, to be an assertion, and so to be an example of sapience, a series of noises must be explicitly criticizable by reference to social norms. Language gets off the ground only when organisms start telling each other that they have made the wrong noise—that that is not the noise one is supposed to make in these circumstances. It gets fully under way only when the organisms are able to tell each other that they have given bad reasons for saying or doing something.

The sort of social norms that make it possible to distinguish good reasons from bad reasons—and thus to be rational—were already in place when a hominid first realized that because she had previously grunted "P," she might well be beaten with sticks if she did not go on to grunt "Q." But the norm only became explicit, and what Brandom calls "the game of giving and asking for reasons" only began, a few hundreds of thousands of years later. At that point, descendants of the original grunters realized that since they have asserted "P" and also asserted "If P then Q," they will be deservedly criticized if they are unable to produce a good reason for refusing to assert "Q."

This Wittgensteinian view can be summed in the claim that there is nothing intermediate between neurons and social practices for either philosophy or cognitive science to study. To study what makes human beings special is to study such practices—to study culture. We neither have nor need a bridge between the neurons and the practices, any more than we need one between hardware and software. Software is just a way of putting hardware to use, and culture is just a way of putting our neurological equipment to use. To understand how hardware works is one thing, but to understand the uses to which it is put is something quite different.

So much for my sketch of the battle lines within contemporary analytic philosophy of mind and language. I hope I have made clear that this is not a battle about alternative solutions to common problems. It is about whether the traditional problems of modern philosophy are to be taken seriously or set aside. As the battle has worn on, it has come to look more and more like a disagreement about what sort of thing philosophers should take themselves to be doing, about the self-image of the discipline. I hope that my account of the matter helps explain why philosophers like Nagel, who still aspire to universalist grandeur, see Wittgenstein and Davidson as cultural disasters.

Philosophical analysis of the sort Russell envisaged requires that there be such things as concepts or meanings that can be isolated and treated as elements of beliefs. But if, as Wittgenstein suggested, a concept is just the use of a word, and if the proper use of the words that interest philosophers is always going to be a matter of controversy, it is not clear how philosophical analysis could possibly help. For a philosopher's claim to have discovered the contours of a concept will always be just a persuasive redefinition of a word. Philosophers' diagnoses of "conceptual confusion" look, from a Wittgensteinian point of view, like disingenuous ways of going about the transformation of culture rather than ways of making clearer what has already been going on.

The same problem arises for beliefs as for meanings. The

anti-Wittgensteinian approach to the matter requires that minds be aggregates of mental representations. But philosophers such as Davidson argue that figuring out what beliefs someone has is not a matter of figuring out which representations are in the "belief box" of her brain but of construing her behavior so as to make as many of her assertions true, and as many of her actions rational, as possible. On the picture common to Wittgenstein and Davidson, we ascribe concepts and beliefs to an organism in order to learn how to cope with her behavior by integrating her projects into our own. The criteria for making these ascriptions are in constant flux because the uses people make of words fluctuate. Such fluctuation is not an undesirable lack of clarity and precision but a desirable ability to adapt to circumstance.

The more holistically we treat the ascription of meaning and belief, the less use we shall have for the notion of "conceptual analysis," or for the claim that cognitive science can help us understand how human beings attain truth. For truth, on Davidson's view, is not the sort of thing that beliefs and assertions can be bumped into having by their encounters with bits of nonlinguistic reality—the sort of encounters in which cognitive scientists specialize. For Davidson, there are no interesting isomorphisms to be discovered between true beliefs and what those beliefs are about—isomorphisms of the sort that Russell and his followers took for granted. So we have to treat "correspondence with reality" as a metaphor that cannot be pressed. Doing so lets us set aside the puzzles that Russell invoked the Fregean notion of logical form in order to resolve.

The thought that Russell and his followers put their discipline on the secure path of a science is very dear to most analytic philosophers, as is the claim that training in analytic philosophy makes for greater conceptual clarity. So one of the reasons Wittgenstein, Sellars, and Davidson are viewed with suspicion is the fear that to take seriously Wittgenstein's suggestion that we should not ask about meaning but only about use is to leave the gates open to obscurantism and sophistry. For if there are no such things as meanings to study, but only the constantly changing uses of words to be traced, there is no such thing as having attained "conceptual clarity."

The philosophers who are willing to give up on the claim that there are such things as "conceptual questions" to be resolved think that philosophy will have to be satisfied with narratives rather than analyses. On their view, the best we can do in the way of understanding how mind and language work is to tell stories, of the sort told by Sellars and Brandom, about how metalinguistic and mentalistic vocabularies came into existence in the course of time, as well as stories about how cultural evolution gradually took over from biological evolution. The latter stories recount how we got out of the woods and into the caverns, out of the caverns and into the villages, and then out of the villages into the law courts and the temples. The kind of understanding that narratives of this sort give us is not the sort that we get from seeing many disparate things as manifestations of the same underlying processes, but rather the sort that comes from expanding our imagination by comparing the social practices of our day with those of past times and possible future times.

Followers of Wittgenstein like myself think that philosophers should give up on the question "What is the place of mental representations, or meanings, or values, in a world of physical particles?" They should regard talk about particles, talk about beliefs, and talk about what ought to be done as cultural activities that fulfill distinct purposes. These activities do not need to be fitted together in a systematic way any more than basketball and cricket need to be fitted together with bridge and chess. If we have a plausible narrative of how we became what we are, and why we use the words we do as we do, we have all we need in the way of self-understanding. We can give up on what Russell called "knowledge as a form of union between Self and not-Self" and stop trying for what Nagel calls an "unconditional context." We can cease to resist Emerson's prophecy that every context, no matter how encompassing, will eventually be subsumed within another, larger, context. We can rejoice in the indefinite expansibility of the human imagination rather than attempting to circumscribe it.

Once one gives up on unconditionality, one will cease to use metaphors of getting down to the hard facts as well as metaphors of looking up toward grand overarching structures. One will start treating hardness as just noncontroversiality. One will begin to wonder, as the older Wittgenstein did, why we ever thought of logic as something sublime. One will instead think of logic as Brandom does—as a device for making our social norms explicit. This shift substitutes horizontal for vertical metaphors of intellectual progress, and thereby abandons the notion that mind or language are things that can be got right once and for all.

As I have already suggested, philosophers who take Hegel seriously substitute questions about what makes us, in our time and place, special for questions about what makes human beings in general special. So it is not surprising that Brandom describes himself as a neo-Hegelian. The more Hegelian philosophy becomes, the more questions about what we share with humans at all other times and places get replaced with questions about how we differ from our ancestors and from our neighbors, and about how our descendants might differ from us. For Hegelians, the most important human activity is not attempting to get things right but reinterpreting and recontexualizing the past—trying to put the past in a new, more imaginative, context.

This difference of opinion about what it is important to think about explains why the Hegel-Nietzsche-Heidegger tradition of nonanalytic philosophy that I have described as "narrative philosophy" is often referred to as "hermeneutic philosophy." The term "hermeneutic" signals a shift of interest from what can be got right once and for all to what can only be reinterpreted and recontextualized over and over again. That is why Brandom's paradigm of rational inquiry is the common law rather than the discovery of physical microstructure. A model which would do as well is literary criticism, whose necessary inconclusiveness is made plain by a remark that Brandom quotes from T. S. Eliot: "What happens when a work of art is created is something that happens simultaneously to all the works of art that preceded it."

Brandom generalizes Eliot's point by saying that Hegel taught us how to think of a concept on the model of a person—as the kind of thing that is understood only when one understands its history. The best answer to a question about who a person really is is a story about her past that provides a context in which to place her recent conduct. Analogously, the most useful response to questions about a concept is to tell a story about the ways in which the uses of certain words have changed in the past, leading up to a description of the different ways in which these words are being used now. The clarity that is achieved when these different ways are distinguished from one another, and when each is rendered intelligible by being placed within a narrative of past usage, is analogous to the increased sympathy we bring to the situation of a person whose life history we have learned.

On the Hegelian view that I have been commending in this lecture, human beings do not have a nature to be understood, but rather a history to be reinterpreted. They do not have a place in a universal scheme of things, nor a special relation to the ruling powers of the universe. But they are capable of increasingly rich and imaginative self-descriptions. They are finite creatures whose latest self-descriptions have shown an increasing willingness to accept that finitude. Tomorrow, in my third lecture, I shall return to the role of the romantic movement in making such willingness possible.

3

ROMANTICISM, NARRATIVE PHILOSOPHY, AND HUMAN FINITUDE

IN YESTERDAY'S LECTURE I DISTINGUISHED BETWEEN ANALYT-ic philosophy and narrative philosophy. I said that analytic philosophers saw human history as a drama unfolding within the confines of the "inclosing wall" that Emerson said did not exist. That wall sets the bounds of the imagination, the limits of coherent speculation. Those limits can be discovered by analyzing the conditions of possibility of language, or knowledge, and of moral deliberation. Narrative philosophers, on the other hand, agree with Emerson that "there is no circumference to us" and with Hegel that philosophy is, at best, its time held in thought. They agree with Wittgenstein that there are no meanings of words to be analyzed, but only uses of words to be described—uses that are, and should be, in constant change. There are no universal and necessary truths to be discovered, but only social practices to be accepted or rejected.

These lectures are themselves examples of narrative philosophy. One of my aims has been to distance you from the problems that non-Wittgensteinian analytic philosophers still take seriously by telling a story about how these problems came into being and how they might be dismantled. The problems in question include those about how things out there in the world make our beliefs and sentences true, about the nature and scope of human knowledge, and about the relation between the mind and the brain. Such questions became salient in the seventeenth century as a result of the rise of corpuscularian natural science, and of what has been called "the mechanization of the world picture." In the course of that century it became clear that Democritus and Lucretius, rather than Plato and Aristotle, had guessed right about how things work. Discussion by writers such as Locke, Spinoza, Hume, and Kant of the problems resulting from this realization played an important part in bringing about the secularization of culture and in preparing the way for the democratic revolutions.

But by the time of Kant those problems had been milked dry. During Kant's lifetime, the attention of the intellectuals was diverted from questions about the relations between science, religion, and morality by the French Revolution and the romantic movement. Hegel was the first of the canonically great philosophers to spot the significance of these two events and to react by substituting History for Nature as the primary datum of philosophical inquiry. By the end of the nineteenth century, most intellectuals, including many philosophy professors, had become convinced that philosophy's function was to help change the future by reinterpreting the past, rather than to offer theories about the intrinsic natures either of human beings or of the really real.

Nevertheless, in some countries the philosophy professors tried to hang on to the pre-Hegelian problematic. Philosophers who took mathematics to be paradigmatic of rational thought—Russell in Britain and Husserl in Germany—still hoped to retain Kant as a model of philosophical inquiry, rather than ceding primacy to Hegel. In the anglophone world, Russell's initiative helped create what we now think of as the "analytic tradition" in philosophy. That tradition tried to revivify the seventeenth-century problematic by shifting philosophy's focus from the relation between consciousness and the extramental reality to that between language and extralinguistic reality.

The linguistic turn, however, made possible a swerve back in the direction of Hegel—a rediscovery of the historicism that Husserl and Russell had hoped to banish from philosophy. The repudiation of empiricism, and, more generally, of representationalism, began with Wittgenstein's *Philosophical Investigations.* The subsequent work of Sellars, Davidson, and Brandom guided anglophone philosophy back to the path that had led German idealism from Kant to Hegel. These developments have led some analytic philosophers to distrust Russell's dictum that "logic is the essence of philosophy" and many nonanalytic philosophers to repudiate Husserl's claim that only the search for apodictic truth can rescue us from irrationalism.

In my first two lectures I emphasized the difference between the aspiration to talk in a wholesale way about the relation between human beings and the cosmos and the aspiration to transcend the human past in order to create a richer human future. I contrasted the traditional logocentric deification of Reason as the faculty that gives us necessity and universality with the romantic apotheosis of the Imagination. In this last lecture I shall try to link up romanticism with pragmatism, and to argue that the two complement one another nicely.

Romanticism tells us that reason would have had nothing to do—that we would have had nothing to think about—had imagination not been at work. Pragmatism tells us that imagination should not be allowed to interfere with reason's activities. Once an activity of reason becomes a social practice, such as mathematics, experimental science, or constitutional jurisprudence, it becomes self-regulating, and should be granted autonomy. It is one thing for an imaginative genius to suggest that we might play a different game, but quite another to disrupt the game presently being played by making illegal moves.

James and Dewey asked us to give up the goal of achieving correspondence with the way things intrinsically are, and to settle for that of leading richer human lives. But that suggestion sounded plausible only because romanticism had already broken the back of Platonism. Isaiah Berlin was right to call romanticism "the deepest and most lasting of all changes in the life of the West." He explains their importance by saying that the romantics were the first to cast doubt on what he calls "the jigsaw puzzle" view of the human situation. Berlin described this view as follows:

> There must be some means of putting these pieces together. The all-wise man, the omniscient being . . . is in principle capable of fitting all the various pieces together into a coherent pattern. Anyone who does this will know what the world is like: what things are, what they have been, what they will be, what the laws are that govern them, what man is, what the relation of man is to things, and therefore what man needs, what he desires, and also how to obtain it.

On the jigsaw puzzle view, philosophy should restrict itself to making current intuitions coherent—intuitions expressible in vocabularies presently available. There is no need for new vocabularies, and thus no role in philosophy for imagination.

One big problem with the jigsaw puzzle view is that it has a hard time accounting for the slow rate of scientific and moral progress. It is puzzling that Aristotle did not hit upon Galilean mechanics, given that the inclined planes and the ballistic trajectories Galileo was to use as evidence for his theories were there for Aristotle's inspection. The Kantian notion of the sources of morality generates a similar puzzle. According to Kant, every human being, at all times and places, has been equally familiar with the moral law. So only what Kant called "radical evil"—knowing the better and doing the worse—can account for Aristotle's endorsement of slavery. On the jigsaw puzzle view, to be rational is simply to have the energy and gumption to put the pieces together, to come to grips with what is already evident. There is no room in such a view for the Kuhnian suggestion that Aristotle and Galileo lived in different worlds, nor for the Marxist suggestion that moralities are products of socioeconomic conditions.

Berlin says that Friedrich Schiller introduced, "for the first time in human thought," the notion that "ideals are not to be discovered at all, but to be invented; not to be found but to be generated as art is generated." As far as I know, none of the romantics went on to say that not only moral and political ideals but also the concepts of natural science and those of common sense were so generated. But I have been arguing in these lectures that all the historicist arguments that can be invoked to back up Schiller's claim about the origin of moral and political concepts can be applied to the origins of these other concepts. In the two hundred or so years since Schiller wrote, historicism has gradually spilled over from moral and political philosophy into philosophy of science, epistemology, and philosophy of language.

The result is the tension I have described between philosophers who search for universal and necessary truth and those who tell stories. Philosophers who remain faithful to the spirit of Russell and Husserl take for granted that philosophy's task is to bring as many as possible of our intuitions into harmony with one another, thus revealing a coherent conceptual structure. This structure fixes the bounds of meaningful discourse; it determines what makes sense and what does not. But for narrative philosophers the problem is not to distinguish sense from nonsense. It is rather to help us understand how what used to be common sense has gradually become almost unintelligible and how what once sounded crazy gradually became uncontroversial.

From the point of view of the founders of analytic philosophy, coherence is the ultimate intellectual virtue. From that of narrative philosophy, coherence and the sort of imaginativeness that gives new uses to old words share the honors. Rationality is indeed a search for the coherence of our beliefs and desires, but imagination keeps proposing new candidates for belief and new things to desire. It keeps adding new pieces to the puzzle, and suggesting that some of the old ones be swept off the table. In the modern West each new generation has found itself confronted with a different puzzle than the one which the previous generation had tried to solve.

The search for stable ahistorical criteria for deciding between competing beliefs and competing desires is a product of the jigsaw puzzle view. If all the pieces of the puzzle are at hand, yet different puzzle solvers still disagree about how they are supposed to fit together, then it would seem that we need criteria for telling a real fit from an apparent fit. The romantics broke dramatically with Platonism by saying that there were no criteria of the desired sort—none that were not themselves subject to imaginative revision. Berlin sums up this accomplishment by saying, "What romanticism did was to undermine the notion that in matters of value, politics, morals, aesthetics there are such things as objective criteria which operate between human beings, such that anyone who does not use these criteria is simply either a liar or a madman, which is true of mathematics or of physics."

In this passage Berlin suggests that mathematics and physics do offer criteria of the described sort. But I think that he would have been willing to concede that even these areas make progress thanks to the imagination of people who are, at first, suspected of insanity. Cantor looked as crazy to many conservative mathematicians as Turner and Cézanne did to many academic artists. Years after his annus mirabilis of 1905, lots of physicists still thought of Einstein as a crank. Berlin would have done better had he simply said that romanticism made us suspect that objective criteria do not drop down from heaven but are themselves historical products. Romanticism suggested that what we call "rational standards" for choosing beliefs and desires are as much up for imaginative grabs as are the vocabularies in which those beliefs and desires are formulated.

Pragmatism and romanticism will seem opposed to one another if we think of the one as urging us to adopt practicality as a criterion and the other telling us that only imaginativeness matters. One can make pragmatism look absurd by describing it as the proposal that we use some version of the utilitarian calculus as a criterion for theory choice or for resolving moral dilemmas. One can make romanticism look silly by thinking of it as an attempt to substitute inspiration for reasoning, or as the claim that authenticity trumps argument. But in these lectures I am trying to make both movements look good by treating them not as constructive proposals but as ways of getting out from under Platonism. Both helped undermine the idea that we can choose between an Aristotelian and a Galilean world picture by applying criteria whose legitimacy would have been obvious to Aristotle, or between the Union and the Confederacy by appealing to a set of moral intuitions shared by both parties to the conflict.

Philosophers who want to hang on to the traditional subjective-objective distinction often dismiss both pragmatism and romanticism as attempts to give the subject the prestige and privileges that properly belong to the object. Heidegger has popularized an account of the shift from Plato and Aristotle to Descartes and Kant as a matter of putting self-hood in the place that substance occupied in Greek thought. Russell, in a passage I quoted yesterday, treats James and Dewey as arguing that the Self should be allowed to dominate the not-Self. But the subjective-objective distinction evaporates when the appearance-reality distinction does. This is because the subject is as much subject to redescription as is the object. The needs of inquirers are as mutable as the terms they use to describe the objects of inquiry. Appeal to those needs no more provides a stable criterion than does appeal to the way things really are. One can change the course of inquiry either by redescribing what one is talking about or by redescribing what one hopes to get out of inquiring about it. This was the point that Dewey made when he spoke of "the means-end continuum." It was a mistake, Dewey argued, to describe deliberation as choosing means to achieve fixed ends, because ends are constantly being reduced to means and means are constantly promoting themselves to the status of ends.

Pragmatists and romantics agree on the futility of attempts to break out of history by describing the point of human existence, or the meaning of human life. To attempt to characterize either means rolling all the diverse activities of which human beings are capable into a homogenous blob— thereby doing the same thing to the subject that Parmenides did to the object. In both cases, we substitute something large, unwieldy, and mysterious for an aggregate of smaller things, each of which we understand reasonably well. Both the meaning of human life and the intrinsic nature of reality are topics about which one can say pretty much anything one likes. Neither can be made a topic of disciplined inquiry. That is why attempts to achieve universalist grandeur tend to degenerate quickly into vacuous bombast.

As I am using the terms "romanticism" and "pragmatism," they are not ways of answering the wholesale questions that Plato posed, but rather reactions against the questions themselves. They are not ways of fulfilling the desires that brought Platonism into existence, but attempts to repress them. Both movements go astray when they succumb to the yearning for grandeur and start claiming to have discovered how things really are.

It is especially important for romantics to guard against such temptations. They have to be careful not to claim the sort of nondiscursive access to truth that was once attributed to seers, shamans, and religious prophets. That is the sort of access that Plato promises to those who are able to clamber up out of the cave and step out into the sunlight. Many philosophers attracted by romanticism invert Plato's vertical metaphors. They say that truth is found by descending into the depths of the human soul. We can make this descent, they suggest, by turning ourselves over to the faculties that Plato stigmatized as "lower"—to will or emotion. They attempt to substitute profundity for grandeur.

But if we are ever to break free of Platonic ways of thinking, we shall have to stop thinking of "reason," "will," "desire," and "emotion" as names of homunculi, striving for control of the body in which they reside. We shall have to abjure the attempt to divide the soul into parts—and the sort of imagery that Plato uses in dialogues such as *Phaedrus*. Such imagery encourages what Berlin calls "the apotheosis of the romantic will." More generally, it facilitates a proliferation of what Jürgen Habermas has called "others to reason"—purported alternative sources of truth such as pure, unconceptualized, prelinguistic experience, or unquestioning religious faith, or mystic rapture, or the mysterious source of insight that Heidegger called *Denken*. Because the philosophical tradition has led us to think of reason as a truth-tracking faculty, doubts about Platonism led post-romantic thinkers to nominate other faculties for this role.

There is, however, no such thing as nondiscursive access to truth. The search for truth cannot be separated from the search for justification. There is no such thing as simply recognizing the truth when you see it—suddenly recollecting what you have always known, deep down inside. For we are not entitled to call our beliefs true unless we can give satisfactory reasons for them, satisfactory by the lights of those whom we accept as rational interlocutors. But to count as such an interlocutor is simply to be someone who plays the same language game we do—someone whose notions of what is relevant to the justification of the belief in question are roughly the same as ours. Romanticism becomes the enemy of progress when it elevates private insight over public justifiability, and becomes contemptuous of consensus. It is one thing to say, with James, that no progress is made unless "individuals of genius show the way." It is another for such individuals to claim to have an inside track to truth, one that exempts them from having to offer reasons for what they say. Shelley's "Defence of Poetry," for example, is an inspired work, but it is also a fine example of argumentative prose.

Once we realize that what counts as a good reason or as a relevant consideration is different in different societies and in different historical epochs, we also realize that being rational is not a matter of putting an innate faculty to use but of conforming to the customs of a particular time and place. The West began to realize this toward the end of the eighteenth century. Herder's cultural relativism helped the romantics realize that the Enlightenment's religion of reason was just as phony as that of the ecclesiastical authorities the philosophes wished to depose. Just as the Church had justified certain social practices by saying that they were the will of God, so the Enlightenment had justified others by saying that they were dictated by reason. Both claims were equally empty.

But once we become historicist enough to realize that the language game we play, and thus our notion of what counts as a good reason, is a result of past contingencies, we may become dubious about the whole idea of having to offer arguments for what we say. We will not make that mistake, however, if we distinguish between rationality as the practice of giving and asking for reasons and rationality as the employment of an innate truth-tracking faculty. To give up on discursive justification would be to give up debating whether to integrate a novelty into our practices. To give up on the notion of a truth-tracking faculty is merely to admit that what counts as discursive justification to one audience will not count as such to another.

Romantics who fail to make this distinction sometimes treat the past as if it were simply a prison from which we need to escape. This sense of imprisonment may then be extended from the language games of the day to language itself. Once we realize that the language games we play are no more inevitable than those played by people whom we regard as primitive or debased, it may be tempting to think that it is language and discursivity themselves that are somehow at fault. So we may start talking about "the prison-house of language," when all we really object to is some particular way of describing some particular phenomena.

Hegel tried to combine historicism with rationalism by proclaiming that the real is the rational, and the rational the real. He out-Platoed Plato by treating Reason as the cunning behind-the-scenes scriptwriter of history. But this attempt to revitalize theodicy collapsed of its own weight. Once historicism got disentangled from Hegelian hyperrationalism, nineteenth-century thinkers like Marx and Spencer began to ask, "If reason does not write the script, what does?" Nietzsche sometimes made the mistake of trying to answer that bad question; when he did so, he apotheosized the will to power. But at his Emersonian best he rejected the question. Heidegger, unfortunately, revived it. He answered it by saying that languages were gifts of Being, conveyed to us by those rare individuals called "Thinkers," the people who wrote the rules for the various language games so far played in the West.

A better reaction to the realization that the Enlightenment had erected a quasi deity called Reason to serve as a surrogate for God would have been to stop looking for a scriptwriter. If post-romantic thinkers had been content to see history as an unplanned series of contingencies, and none the worse for that, they would have been able to substitute what Habermas calls "a communicative conception of reason" for a "subject-centered" conception. Putting Habermas's point in Wittgensteinian terms, they would have stopped thinking of Reason as the name either of a faculty or of a guiding power and started thinking of it simply as the practice of giving and asking for reasons.

Where I differ from Habermas is that he thinks it important to see this practice as aiming at universal validity. In various exchanges between us, I have argued that universal validity is a notion that does not work. I do not see that it can be made relevant to practice. Whereas I am happy to admit that adopting a social-practice conception of rationality requires us to relativize what counts as "the better argument," Habermas finds such relativization debilitating. But his insistence that the regulative ideal of universal validity can save us from relativism seems to me inconsistent with his own account of reason as communicative rather than subject centered. I cannot see how, given this account, he can still maintain what amounts to an immanent teleology, one that insures that sociopolitical freedom will insure the triumph of the better argument—"better" in a universalistic, unrelativized sense.

I see such an immanent teleology as the last vestige of the idea that history follows a script. On the view I put forward in my first lecture, imagination is not a candidate for the role of scriptwriter. It is neither a homunculus nor any other sort of agent. To say that imagination is prior to reason is just to say that somebody has to think up things to talk about, to envisage the outlines of a novel social practice, to walk as the prophecy of the next age, before progress can occur. The imagination is not a means of access to truth, but rather to novelty—novelty whose adoption may or may not be a good thing.

Hitler had as powerful an imagination as Pericles or Jefferson. Mao Tse-tung's fantasies were as attractive as those of St. Paul. The new social practice that is put in place as a result of somebody's poetic vision may be a very bad practice indeed. But if we give up on the Platonic and Kantian notion of an innate ability to tell visions that will produce good from those that will produce evil, we can still say that if nobody has any visions, nothing will ever get any better than it is now.

This is merely to say that experience is our only teacher when it comes to deciding which new proposals to dismiss as fantasy and which to praise as imaginative. If we can cease to feel the urge that drove Plato, the urge to rise above the ambiguous lessons of accumulated experience and to find ahistorical criteria by which to justify our decisions, we can combine Shelley's ebullient praise of the imagination with Dewey's sober insistence that moral and political progress will always require willingness to make dangerous experiments.

Whereas romanticism reminds us that imagination may produce a human future that is wonderfully different from the human present, pragmatism reminds us that the only sure test of utility is, unfortunately, retrospective—whether we, by the lights of our own time and place, are grateful to those who came up with the novel idea. If we could test for an idea's utility in advance of trying it out in practice, there would be no need for risky experimentation. But a world in which that risk is absent would be one in which we were not the finite, time-bound creatures that we are.

If there were criteria of the sort that Plato claimed were available, St. Paul's auditors should have been able to apply them and discover whether Christianity is, as some of its defenders have claimed, the most rational of religions or, as Kierkegaard argued, the most irrational. We should also have been able to test Marxism's claim to be the most scientific of political theories, and Mussolini's claim that parliamentary democracy was incompatible with social justice. But in fact we had to wait for people to put Christian, Marxist, and fascist ideas to use before we could be sure what, if anything, they were good for. We had to experiment with them and see how they worked out. All of us think it would have been better if nobody had ever experimented with fascism. Many of us think we should not have experimented with Marxism. Nietzsche regretted that Christianity was not nipped in the bud. But nobody can deny that we learned a lot from watching all three sets of ideas be put into practice.

Just as romanticism is a philosophy of unbounded hope, so pragmatism is a philosophy of finitude. Romanticism tells us that past experience is insufficient to show the impossibility of change for the better—that the results of past experiments should not discourage us from trying new ones. Pragmatism tells us that we shall never know for sure whether what now looks like progress is actually regression. Romanticism encourages us to transcend the present by walking as the prophecies of the next age. Pragmatism reminds us that there is no intrinsic value in novelty—that the only test of prophecy is whether the new age turns out to be an improvement on the old.

To acknowledge human finitude is simply to grant there is no way of knowing, at any given moment in history, whether humanity is heading in the right direction. The pursuit of criteria which transcend the social practices of a time and place is an attempt to evade this finitude. So is the attempt to philosophize at a wholesale level—to say something general about the relation between social institutions and human nature, or between the various things that different sorts of men and women have found valuable and The Good Life for Man.

Critics of pragmatism have often said that if we give up the attempt to think in a wholesale way, we are betraying something essential to our humanity. The point of being human, these critics say, is to have a reach that exceeds our grasp. But there is a difference between retail sociopolitical goals that we may never succeed in realizing and wholesale philosophical ideals. All of us here believe that we have a duty to work for a future in which the entire population of the planet will have freedom and the security that the middle classes of Europe and North America presently enjoy. None of us are clear about how this can be done, any more than ancient Roman idealists were clear about how the work of the world could get done if slavery were abolished. But there is considerable agreement among us on what counts as a step in the right direction, and we share the hope that a sequence of such steps will, sooner or later, achieve the desired end. There is no such agreement when it comes to wholesale ideals like "universal validity" or "the achievement of true happiness" or "the fulfillment of God's plan" or "the rule of reason." A retail ideal is one that we can put to work. But the only function of a wholesale ideal is to puff ourselves up, to give us the sense that we are associated with something that does not share our finitude.

Perhaps the best way to wrap up what I have been saying in these lectures is to turn to the question, What would intellectual life be like if the Platonic search for ahistorical criteria came to seem as quaint as the worship of the Olympian deities? If retail ideals were the only ones thought worthy of discussion? If human finitude, and the priority of the imagination to reason, were taken for granted? If romanticism and pragmatism had both come to seem simple common sense? If the jigsaw puzzle view of things had come to seem as implausible as the notion of divine providence?

In the past I have sometimes described such a culture as one in which literature and the arts have replaced science and philosophy as sources of wisdom. But that description now seems to me misguided. I think it would be better to say that it would be a culture in which the meaning of the word "wisdom" had reverted to its pre-Platonic sense. Before the Greek word *sophia* acquired the special sense that Socrates and Plato gave it, it meant something like "skill," something that could be gained only through the accumulation of experience. In that older sense, wisdom can be gained only by living a long time, seeing many men and cities, and keeping one's eyes open. But after Socrates and Plato it was thought of differently; *sophia* came to mean getting in touch with something that was not the product of experience at all. The Greek word for "love of wisdom," *philosophia,* which had once meant something like "intellectual culture," came to denote the attempt to escape from finitude, to get in touch with the eternal, to achieve some sort of transcendence of the merely human.

In a culture that had given up on Platonism, it would be history rather than science, philosophy, art, or literature that would be central to intellectual life. The accumulated experience of the race, as recorded by historians, offers to each new human generation the same benefits that conversation with those who have lived long and seen much offers to the young. History will become central just insofar as intellectuals no longer attempt to see things under the aspect of eternity. The closest they would come to such an attempt would be to offer summaries of the lessons of human experience so far—the sort of summary that Hegel attempted.

Once Hegel's claim that philosophy is its time held in thought is detached from theodicy, philosophy becomes a matter of understanding how present actualities emerged out of earlier actualities, rather than attempting to specify Kantian "conditions of possibility." Instead of asking how experience, or knowledge, or language is possible, Hegelians ask why it took this particular form rather than that at a particular time and place. Insofar as philosophy is an attempt at synoptic vision, therefore, it must take the form of a supernarrative—a story that holds the history of science together with that of politics, history of poetry together with that of theology, the sequence of canonical philosophical texts together with that of canonical works of architecture.

Providing such a synoptic vision sounds like too big an assignment for a single thinker, and of course it is. Hegel was the first even to make a stab at composing such a supernarrative, and even he, with all his gifts and all his courage, left behind only some scribbled sketches. It would be absurd to suggest that the academic discipline of philosophy should reshape itself so that every philosophy professor attempts to write such a supernarrative. But there is no reason to identify the activity that is at the center of intellectual life with the province of a specialized academic discipline. The attempt to get as much profit as possible from the accumulated experience of the species cannot be the product of specialized, quasi-scientific inquiry. It cannot be conducted systematically or rigorously. So in a post-Platonic culture, the love of wisdom would revert to its older sense of "intellectual culture."

The pre-Hegelian idea of philosophy as a sort of superdiscipline—queen of the sciences, arbiter of rationality, and drawer of cultural boundaries—has never been very plausible. When philosophy starts giving itself airs of this sort, it is usually because somebody is claiming to have discovered a marvelous new truth-tracking methodology—such as Descartes's technique for separating the clear and distinct from the opaque and fuzzy, or what Kant called "transcendental reflection," or what Russell described as "logical analysis," or Husserl as "eidetic reduction." But such announcements are merely rhetorical devices for changing the subject.

Once one brushes this sort of rhetoric aside, what the philosophers I have mentioned are really saying is, "Pose the issues in my terms, rather than in those used by my predecessors; problems posed in their terms are pseudoproblems, whereas I have discovered the real problems of philosophy."

Each of these philosophers had a novel idea about what philosophy could be, an idea that caught on and helped create a school of philosophical thought—people who talked the master's talk, took his newly formulated problems seriously, and glossed his texts intensively. But from Descartes and Locke to Russell and Husserl the effect of each such new idea has been to increase the isolation of philosophy from the rest of culture. The more professional the discipline has become, the less use nonphilosophers have had for it. The present hyperprofessionalization of analytic philosophy, and its almost complete invisibility to the rest of the intellectual world, is only the latest stage of a process that began when Aristotle was translated into Latin in the thirteenth century. His medieval admirers were quick to claim that a mastery of Aristotelian jargon was a prerequisite for the acquisition of wisdom.

Philosophy, as the saying goes, always buries its undertakers. This is true, in the sense that the attempt to achieve a synoptic vision of human achievements will never cease. But the idea of an academic discipline devoted to achieving such a vision may be on its way out. So I hope it is clear that I am not proposing that professors of history try to wrest a delusional primacy from their colleagues in the philosophy department. The role of specialist in things in general should be left vacant.

Rather, I am suggesting that our culture is gradually becoming one in which to call an intellectual "wise" no longer means that she has got in touch with something that is more than just a product of the human imagination, something immune to redescription. It is coming to mean instead that she combines a desirable openness to novel proposals with familiarity with the fates that have overtaken many past proposals. Such people recognize that although the only hope for the future lies in the human imagination, novelty alone is never a sufficient recommendation. A combination of romanticism and pragmatism lets them see the relation between the human present and the human past as analogous to the relation between earlier and later stages of individual development: there is no immanent teleology in either case, but that does not make experiments in individual or social living less necessary or less meaningful.

If we can avoid the fallacy of thinking either that the contingency of a social practice implies that it should be dropped or that the sheer novelty of a suggested practice is sufficient reason to adopt it, then intellectual life will survive the collapse of the appearance-reality distinction, as well as the relativization of rationality. The combination of romanticism and pragmatism that I have been suggesting in these lectures will seem as plausible and uncontroversial to the intellectuals of the future as the quest for universalist grandeur and transcultural rationality has seemed to the past. Those future intellectuals will not be closer to the way things really are than Plato was, but their imaginations will be dominated by a different sense of what it is to be human—one that takes our finitude for granted rather than attempting to escape from it.

AFTERWORD

MARY V. RORTY

H E READ A LOT, THAT MAN. HE STARTED EARLY, AND he kept it up.

Seeing where it took him, it's easy to suspect that he persisted in philosophy after his (very) early years at Robert Hutchins's University of Chicago because, of all possible majors, it was the one least likely to restrict the range of things he could justify reading. But he read not just out of antiquarian affection for the best that has been thought and said—but also with constant attention to the implications of what he read for our time, our moment in history. And he read—and wrote—because of his conviction that words matter, that our language is our world, and that by our words we can change our world.

I don't think anyone ever doubted that he had in fact read all the people whose names fill the pages of his writings, and the scrawling marginalia in his library attest to the attention he gave their work—whether or not his construals of what they meant were uncontroversial. In these three lectures, for instance, he drops twenty-seven names in the first lecture, thirty-seven in the third, and a resounding forty-two names in the second—although, to soften the blow, it's usually the same names in each. One of the nice things about his cavalier division of the history of philosophy into heroes and villains, and one of the things that helps his international reputation, is that if you aren't familiar with what separates Pierce and Dewey, or the different priorities of Russell and Wittgenstein, you may nonetheless appreciate his view of what divides Husserl from Heidegger, and thus get a sense of the party for which he wants your allegiance. It is often with American pragmatism, under some—his?—description, a commodious tent, into which he was inclined to drag many contemporaries who might have had little inclination to enter it voluntarily.

What strikes me about the Page-Barbour lectures—and indeed about much of his later work—is his vision of philosophy as one form of literature, a novel, rather than a mere biography, about the life of some ideas, tracing the convoluted growth and transformations of concepts over the course of time. In the third lecture he finally gave me a source—Hegel—for one of his deepest convictions: that "philosophy is, at best, its time held in thought." To hold late-twentieth-century philosophy in thought means to acknowledge its ancestry and its variety—and to suggest a direction for its future development, as well. Ambitious? Hmm. Controversial? I'd hope so. It is, after all, our disagreements that keep us reading our peers and writing about them.

Revisiting the Page-Barbour lectures Richard gave at the University of Virginia in the early years of the twenty-first century evokes pleasant memories of the time the family spent in Charlottesville—civility, collegiality, and the kind of intellectual stimulation and freedom that only a great university can provide. He was surprised, I think—even puzzled—by the impact of the publication of *Mirror of Nature* in 1979 on some of his most valued colleagues and friends; why, and how, could they take this odyssey of an idea so personally? The offer of a university professorship from UVa in 1981 offered a safe harbor of sorts: he could go to two department meetings (or neither); anything the English department didn't like they could blame on the influence of the philosophy department, and vice versa. One of his heroes (second only to P. G. Wodehouse), the British humorist Stephen Potter, recommended in his book *The Theory and Practice of Gamesmanship* that the wise man would be a member not of one club, but of two, so that he could "be the other in the other"—wear a beret to the Guards, a topee to the Arts. A transdepartmental university professorship, he figured, was the best thing since the invention of tenure. His post-emeritus move to Stanford at the turn of the century offered many of the same advantages.

Some of his most enduring friendships—and mine— were formed in our decades in Charlottesville. The philosophy department and women's studies welcomed the participation in their programs of a faculty wife; the medical school, to my amusement, was offering a master's in clinical ethics that encouraged philosophers to add some practical experience to their theory. The idea that philosophy could and should intervene in the world—in as many ways as possible, rather than only as a cloistered academic pursuit—was an idea dear to any Rortyan heart.

There is a certain justice in titling this collection of Rorty's Page-Barbour lectures "Philosophy as Poetry." For a man as logocentric as Richard, it is easy to think in genres, and certainly he considered philosophy as one literary genre among others—as are physics, or mathematics, or medicine, all representing ways of finding (or imposing) order on the chaos of the world around us, so we could talk about it to each other. His last publication was a short piece for *Poetry* magazine, titled "The Fire of Life." Speaking of the pleasure he took in the poems he had consigned to memory, he wrote that he wished he had spent more of his reading time stocking his head with verses to which he could turn at leisure. If philosophy is poetry, then perhaps, when changing how you describe things changes the world, poetry is also philosophy.

INDEX

abstract, the, 5

"Against Theory" (Knapp and Michaels), xix

analytic philosophy, 23–42; on coherence as ultimate intellectual virtue, 48; on "conceptual confusion" diagnosis, 37; Continental philosophy contrasted with, 26–34; "Determinacy Debate" and, xx; on Hegel and Heidegger as not really doing philosophy, 30; internal debate in, 34–42; linguistic turn, 45; narrative philosophy distinguished from, 39–40, 43–44, 47–48; on ontology, 3; problems still taken seriously in, 43–44; professionalization of, 61; Rorty as apostate for, xvii–xviii; Rorty as thinking in both analytic and Continental traditions, xviii; Russell in origins of, 45; on science as model for philosophy, 32, 38–39; seen as intellectual cowards, 30. *See also* Wittgensteinians

Anaxagoras, 3

animal language, xxiv–xxv

appearance-reality distinction, 1–22; benefits of abandoning, xxvii, 1; in common sense, 1, 3, 9; as having outlived its usefulness, xxii–xxiii, 19; intellectual life will survive collapse of, 62; Nietzsche's polemic against, 9–10, 19, 31; in Platonism, viii, 1, 2, 31; in secular world, xxix; subjective-objective distinction and, 50

Aquinas, Thomas, 23

Aristotle: cultural function of philosophy of, 23; and Galilean mechanics, 47, 49–50; guessed wrong about how things work, 44; Heidegger on shift from Greek philosophy to Descartes and Kant, 50; medieval view of, 61; on sense perception as representation, 11; slavery endorsed by, 47

Auden, W. H., xxi

Augustine, St., 35

Austin, John, 24

Ayer, A. J., 24

Beck, Ulrich, 26

Being, 2

Being and Time (Heidegger), x–xvi

belief: analyzing in terms of mind-brain identity, 35; coherence of, 48; as cultural activity, 39–40; justified, 2; in Russell's type of philosophical analysis, 37; Wittgensteinians on, 34, 37–38

Bergson, Henri, 24

Berkeley, George, 28

Berlin, Isaiah, 46, 47, 48–49, 52
Birth of Tragedy, The (Nietzsche), 7
Bloom, Harold, ix–x
Brandom, Robert: on being an
    assertion, xxv, 36; in debates
    within analytic philosophy,
    25; guides in rediscovery of
    historicism, 45; on logic, 40;
    as narrative philosopher, 39;
    as neo-Hegelian, 40; paradigm
    for rational inquiry of, 41; on
    prelinguistic awareness, 17–18;
    Rorty draws from, 11

Cantor, Georg, ix, 49
Caputo, John, xvi
Carnap, Rudolf, xviii, 24
Cassirer, Ernst, 24
causal relations, 16
Cézanne, Paul, 49
Christianity, 56
"Circles" (Emerson), 6–7
cognitive science: holistic accounts
    of meaning and belief and, 38;
    on mind-brain identity, 35; on
    sense perception, 11; in split in
    analytic philosophy, 18, 34
coherence, 48
common sense: appearance-reality
    distinction and, 1, 3, 9; Hegel
    and Heidegger and, 28; if
    romanticism and pragmatism
    seemed as simple as, 58; as
    invented not discovered, 47;
    Nietzsche and, 9; what used to
    be becomes unintelligible, 48
concepts: conceptual analysis, 38;
    conceptual questions, 39; em-
    piricism on, 11, 12; Hegel on,
    41; as invented not discovered,
    47; most useful response to

questions about, 41; Wittgen-
    stein on, 12, 37, 39, 43
concrete, the, 5
Consequences of Pragmatism
    (Rorty), xxvii–xxviii
Continental philosophy: analytic
    philosophy contrasted with,
    26–34; Rorty as thinking in
    both analytic and Continental
    traditions, xviii. *See also* narra-
    tive philosophy
Contingency, Irony, and Solidarity
    (Rorty), xvi
Copernicus, Nicolaus, 23
corpuscularian natural science, 44
correspondence theory of truth,
    38, 46
Crews, Frederick, ix
culture: cultural evolution, 35–36,
    39; cultural relativism, 53;
    meaning as cultural activity,
    39–40; philosophy's cultural
    role, 23–24; philosophy seen as
    drawer of cultural boundaries,
    60; secularization of, xxvi, 44;
    transcultural rationality, 62; as
    way of putting our neurological
    equipment to use, 37

Dante, 23
Darwin, Charles, xxii
Davidson, Donald: on belief, 38;
    on commonly accepted truths,
    2–3; in debates within analytic
    philosophy, 25; versus Fodor,
    24; guides in rediscovery of
    historicism, 45; on language,
    xxv; philosophers who aspire to
    universalist grandeur versus, 37,
    39; on prelinguistic awareness,
    17–18; Rorty draws from,

11; and Rorty thinking in both analytic and Continental traditions, xviii; on Russell's theory of descriptions, 28; on truth, 38

deconstruction, xviii, xix, 3

"Defence of Poetry" (Shelley), xxix, 7, 52

democracy, 44, 56

Democritus, 3, 44

Derrida, Jacques, xv, xvii, xviii

Descartes, René, 14, 17, 35, 50, 60, 61

"Determinacy Debate" (Rorty and Hirsch), xix–xx, xxi

Dewey, John, xv, 46, 50, 56, 64

direct awareness, 21

Dworkin, Ronald, 26

Eckhart, Meister, 21

eidetic reduction, 60

Einstein, Albert, 49

Eliot, T. S., 41

Emerson, Ralph Waldo: "Circles," 6–7; on endlessly expanding circles, 6, 20, 29; on every context being subsumed by another, 40; Nietzsche compared with, 10; on "no inclosing wall," 6, 21, 34, 43; on romantic view of progress, 6–7, 21

empiricism: antiempiricist view of mind, 11–15; British, 8, 21; on concepts as representations, 11, 12; direct awareness in, 21; on language learning, 12, 17; repudiation of, 45; on sense perception, 11, 20

Enlightenment, 7, 45, 53, 54

epistemology: as core area of philosophy, 25; historicism in, 47;

naturalized, 32. *See also* belief; knowledge

experimentalism, 24

faculty psychology, 4

fantasy: imagination contrasted with, xxiii, 4; new practices that are dismissed as, 56

fascism, 56

finitude: acceptance of, 42, 57; expressing in terms of better ways of being human, xxii, 1; Hegel's hope of transcending human, 17; philosophy attempts to escape from, 59; possibility of access to the Real and, 2, 25; pragmatism's acceptance of, xxvi, 57; Rorty on limitations of human, viii; taking it for granted, 58, 62

"Fire of Life, The" (Rorty), 65–66

Fodor, Jerry, 17–18, 24

Foucault, Michel, xviii

Fraser, Nancy, 26

freedom: for everyone, 57; imagination as source of, 13; sociopolitical, 55

Frege, Gottlob: Heidegger contrasted with, 32; hoped to make things clearer, xx–xxi, 28; on logical form, 27, 38; on Plato on what makes human beings special, 30

Freud, Sigmund, xvii, xxi

Gadamer, Hans-Georg, 24

Galileo, 23, 47, 49–50

Gay Science, The (Nietzsche), 8–9

Habermas, Jürgen, xviii, 24, 26, 52, 54–55

Hegel, Georg Wilhelm Friedrich: absolute idealism of, 17; attempts to combine historicism with rationalism, 54; attempts to compose supernarrative, 60; on concepts, 41; as first philosopher to see importance of French revolution and romantic movement, 44; as hermeneutic philosopher, 41–42; historicism of, ix, 17, 44, 54; hoped to make things different, xxi, 28–29, 44; on humans drawing successively wider circles around themselves, 31; on nature as moment in development of Spirit, 10; as not really doing philosophy, according to analytic philosophers, 30; out-Platoed Plato, 54; *The Phenomenology of Spirit,* 26–27; on philosophy as its time held in thought, 43, 59, 64; on putting the past in a new, more imaginative context, 40–41; on requests for definitions and premises, 29; on universalist grandeur, 32

Heidegger, Martin: *Being and Time,* x–xvi; versus Cassirer, 24; on *Denken,* 52; Hegelian historicism reformulated by, 17; as hermeneutic philosopher, 41; hoped to make things different, xxi, 28–29; versus Husserl, 64; on language, 29, 54; *Letter on Humanism,* 26; on Nietzsche as last metaphysician, 10; as not really doing philosophy, according to analytic philosophers, 30; Platonic logocentrism in,

xviii; on requests for definitions and premises, 29; on romantic poets, xxix; Rorty's indifference to late, xv, xvi; Rorty's seminar on, x–xvi, xxiv; and Russell's theory of descriptions, 28; on shift from Greek philosophy to Descartes and Kant, 50; on universalist grandeur, 32; on what makes human beings special, 31–32

Herder, Johann Gottfried von, 17, 53

hermeneutic philosophy, 41–42

Hirsch, E. D., xix–xx, xxi

historicism: of Hegel, ix, 17, 44, 54; Nagel on, 33; rediscovery of, 45; of Schiller, 47; on what counts as a good reason, 53

Holbo, John, xxvi–xxvii

"How Relevant Is 'Postmodern' Philosophy to Politics?" (Rorty), ix

human rights, 5, 24

Hume, David, 21, 32, 44

Husserl, Edmund, 44, 45, 48, 60, 61, 64

Hutchins, Robert, 63

idealism: absolute, 17; German, 8, 18–19, 45; idealist metaphysics, 6, 7; linguistic, 5–6; Roman, 58; transcendental, 17; what is true in, 16

ideals: as invented not discovered, 47; moral and political, 47; retail versus wholesale, 58. *See also* idealism

imagination: analytic philosophy on enclosing, 43; expanding, 18, 34, 39, 40; fantasy contrasted with, xxiii, 4; Hegel as putting the past in a new, more imaginative context, 40–41; imaginative redescription, 7–8, 13–14, 20; imaginative self-description, 41; in jigsaw puzzle view of human situation, 46; in mathematics and physics, 49; on new candidates for belief, 48; new practices that are judged imaginative, 56; as not distinctively human, 15; our ancestors' versus our own, xxii, 1; Plato on substituting application of criteria for, 20, 56; poetic, 3; pragmatism on, 45–46; priority over reason, 9, 15, 25, 45, 55, 58; romantics on, 7, 13, 45, 56; Shelley on, 7, 13, 56; as source of language, 13, 15; wisdom and, 61

immanent teleology, 55, 62

ineffable, the, viii, 21

"In Memory of Sigmund Freud" (Auden), xxi

irony, xxiv

James, William: correspondence view rejected by, 46; Nagel reacts against, 33; on progress, 6, 7, 52; Russell reacts against, 32, 50

jigsaw puzzle view of human situation, 46–47, 48, 58

justification, 2, 52, 53

Kant, Immanuel: analytic philosophers retain him as model for philosophy, 44–45; on conditions of possibility, 59; cultural function of philosophy of, 23;

Heidegger on shift from Greek philosophy to, 50; on innate ability to evaluate visions, 55; on inseparability of things from our thoughts of them, 17; Nietzsche on goal of, 8; on problems resulting from corpuscularian natural science, 44; questions scope and limits of human knowledge, 31–32; seen as failing to recognize language as medium in which humans represent reality to themselves, 30; on sources of morality, 47; on thing-in-itself, 9, 16; on transcendental reflection, 60

Kierkegaard, Søren, 56

Knapp, Steven, xix

knowledge: conditions of possibility of, 43, 59; Hegel on, 10; and identification, 14–15; increased, 5; language as required for, xxiv–xxv, 12, 13; nondiscursive, 20–21; objective, viii; physics seen as paradigmatic form of, ix, 32; Plato on opinion versus, 2, 20; questioning scope and limits of, 31–32, 44; Russell on, 33, 40; the unrelatable as unknowable, 21

Kuhn, Thomas, xv–xvi, xxii, 47

language: access to reality unmediated by, 3–4; animal, xxiv–xxv; beaver dams compared with, xxiii, xxv, 4–5; conditions of possibility of, 43, 59; contingency of all languages, xxiv; fitting into physicalistic world picture, 32; Heidegger on, 29, 54; imagination as source of,

language (*continued*)
13, 15; importance of assent or criticism in, viii, xxiii, xxv, xxvii, 12–13, 36; linguistic turn in philosophy, 45; as medium in which humans represent reality to themselves, 30; naming, 12, 17; nothing outside to which it attempts to become adequate, 7; as not something that can be got right once and for all, 40; prelinguistic awareness, 17–18; "prison-house of language" view, 53–54; rationality and, viii, xxiii, xxv, 4, 15; as relational, 21; social practice account of, 4, 25, 34, 35–37; talking about in ways consistent with science, 35; traditional account of learning, 12, 17; Wittgensteinians on, 34; Wittgenstein on concepts as uses of words, 12, 37, 39, 43; the world seen as constituted by, 15–16. *See also* language games; meaning; philosophy of language

language games: geniuses suggesting new or disrupting that presently being played, 46; Heidegger on those who wrote the rules for, 54; rationality as making allowed moves within, 15, 25; as result of past contingencies, 53; in what makes a rational interlocutor, 52

Letter on Humanism (Heidegger), 26

Letters on the Aesthetic Education of Man (Schiller), 9

Life as Jamie Knows It (Bérubé),

xxiv, xxviii
literature: philosophy as form of, 64, 65; as replacing philosophy, 58. *See also* poetry

Locke, John, 11, 44, 61

logic: as essence of philosophy for Russell, 45; logical analysis, 60, 61; logical form, 27, 30, 38; Wittgenstein on, 40

logocentrism, xviii, 45, 65

Losh, Liz, ix

Lucretius, 44

Manent, Pierre, 26

Marx, Karl, 23, 54

Marxism, 47, 56

materialism, 24

mathematics, 44, 46, 49, 65

meaning: analyzing in terms of mind-brain identity, 35; as cultural activity, 39–40; determinacy of, xix–xx; of human life, 50–51; in Russell's type of philosophical analysis, 37; seeking bounds of, 48; Wittgensteinians on, 34, 37–38; Wittgenstein on uses of words versus, 12, 37, 39

means-end continuum, 50

metaphysics: as core area of philosophy, 25; idealist, 6, 7; Nietzsche on postmetaphysical age, 10; ontology, 3–4; quarrels about nature of Reality in, 3

Michaels, Walter Benn, xix

Mill, John Stuart, 8, 14, 23

mind, the: and brain, 35, 44; Cartesian picture of, 14, 17; fitting into physicalistic world picture, 32; as not something that can be got right once and for all,

40; as possession of certain social skills, 12–13; prelinguistic awareness, 17–18; social practice account of, 25, 34, 35–37; talking about in ways consistent with science, 35; the world seen as dependent on, 16. *See also* cognitive science; philosophy of mind; thought

Mirror of Nature (Rorty), 64–65

morality: conditions of moral deliberation, 43; Kant on sources of, 47; moral ideals, 47; moral progress, xxii, 56; moral purity, 23; romanticism on, 48–49

multiculturalism, x

Mussolini, Benito, 56

mysticism, 21, 52

Nachlass (Nietzsche), 9, 14

Nagel, Thomas, 33–34, 37, 40

naming, 12, 17

narrative philosophy: analytic philosophy distinguished from, 39–40, 43–44, 47–48; on coherence, 48; as hermeneutic philosophy, 41; Rorty on Wittgenstein and, xxi

Newton, Isaac, xvi, 13–14, 15, 18

Nietzsche, Friedrich: antiempiricism of, 12; on appearance-reality distinction, 9–10, 19, 31; on being and identification, 14–15, 16, 21; *The Birth of Tragedy,* 7; on Christianity, 56; and Emerson's metaphor of expanding circles, 20; as first philosopher to be free from illusion, 10; as hermeneutic philosopher, 41; inverted Platonism attributed to, xviii, 10;

Nachlass, 9, 14; on nature as a poem, 8, 11, 18; on philosophy and poetry, 7–9; on Platonism, 2, 7–8, 10, 19, 25, 31; on religion as escapism, 25; on science seen through optic of art, 18, 19; *Twilight of the Gods,* 19; on universalist grandeur, 32; what is true in idealism preserved by, 16; on what makes human beings special, 31; on will to power, 10, 54

novelty: arts and sciences derive from, 5; Hegel and Heidegger as open to, xxi; imagination and, xxiii, 4, 15; integrating into our practices, 53; novel social practice, 55–56; philosophers have novel ideas, 60; on progress, 57; sheer, 62; true test of utility as retrospective, 56; wisdom and openness to, 61

objectivity: Nagel on, 33; objective criteria, 48–50; philosophy seen as search for, viii, xxii; subjective-objective distinction, 50

One, the, 2

ontology, 3–4

Parmenides, 2, 7–8, 19, 50

Paul, St., 56

Peirce, Charles Sanders, 64

persuasion, 4, 13, 15, 37

Phaedrus (Plato), 51–52

Phenomenology of Spirit, The (Hegel), 26

Philosophical Investigations (Wittgenstein), 45

philosophy: "conceptual confu-

philosophy (*continued*)
sion" diagnosis in, 37; core areas of, 25; cultural function of, 23–24; heroes and villains of Rorty, 64; history replacing in a culture that had given up Platonism, 59, 61; increasing isolation from rest of culture, 61; intervening in the world, 65; as its time held in thought for Hegel, 43, 59, 64; in jigsaw puzzle view of human situation, 46; keeping a civil conversation going, xvi–xvii, xx; as literature, 64, 65; literature and the arts replacing, 58; as love of wisdom, 59, 60; origins of Western, 2; poetry as, 66; poetry's quarrel with, 3, 7–9, 20, 21, 24–25; politics and, xxi–xxii; "post-Philosophical society," xxvii–xxviii; pre-Hegelian idea of, 60–61; "problems of," 24; as problem-solving, xv; professionalization of, 61; pseudoproblems in, viii; role of specialist of things in general should be left vacant, 61; as science, 32, 38–39; as search for "Truth," viii, xxii; seen as epistemological physics, ix, 32; as set of tools to work for human betterment, xxiii; social and political, 25–26, 47; as supernarrative, 59–60; taking the conflict down a notch, xxvi; unmediated access to reality sought by, 3–4; at wholesale level, 57–58. *See also* analytic philosophy; Continental philosophy; narrative philosophy;

and branches of philosophy and philosophers by name

philosophy of language: analytic, 26; as core area of philosophy, 25; historicism in, 47; split in analytic philosophy regarding, 34–37

philosophy of mind: analytic, 26; as core area of philosophy, 25; split in analytic philosophy regarding, 34–37

philosophy of science, 47

physics, ix, 32, 49, 65

Platonism: allegory of the cave, 20, 51; antiempirical view criticized by, 17; appearance-reality distinction in, viii, 1, 2, 31; aspiration to universalist grandeur, 34; contemporary philosophical disagreement over, 25; cultural function of, 23; divided line, 20; guessed wrong about how things work, 44; Hegel out-Platoed Plato, 54; Heidegger on shift from Greek philosophy to Descartes and Kant, 50; on immaterial entities, 17; on innate ability to evaluate visions, 55; logocentrism in, xviii; on mind as wax tablet, 11; Nietzsche's inverted, xviii, 10; Nietzsche's opposition to, 2, 7–8, 10, 19, 25, 31; *Phaedrus,* 51–52; post-Platonic culture, 60; pragmatism and romanticism as ways of getting out from under, 49, 51; pragmatism versus, xxvi; on progress, 21; on reaching a place beyond hypotheses, 20; romanticism breaks back of, 46; search for ahistorical criteria,

58–59; soul divided into parts in, 51–52; on ways of speaking and access to the really real, 28; on what makes human beings special, 30–32; on wisdom, 58, 59

Plotinus, 21

poetry: answer to a great poem is a still greater poem, 19; nature as a poem, 8, 11, 18; in philosophical supernarrative, 59; as philosophy, 66; philosophy's quarrel with, 3, 7–9, 20, 21, 24–25; poetic imagination, 3; poets as unacknowledged legislators of the world, xxix, 9, 18; romantic poets and secularization, xxix; Shelley enlarges meaning of "poetry," 7; Shelley's "Defence of Poetry," xxix, 7, 52

politics: contemporary serious political arguments, 24; in philosophical supernarrative, 59; political ideals, 47; political progress, 56; Rorty on philosophy and, xxi–xxii; social and political philosophy, 25–26, 47

positivism, xi, 3, 17

Posner, Richard, 26

postmodern relativists, 24–25, 33

poststructuralism, vii, xv

Potter, Stephen, 65

pragmatism: analytic philosophers on, 32–34; anti-representationalism of, ix; combining romanticism with, 61–62; as commodious tent, 64; Heidegger's *Being and Time* and, x–xv; on imagination, 45–46; on ontology, 3; as

philosophy of finitude, 57; in process of secularization, xxvi; on progress, 57; realism versus, xxviii; romanticism compared with, 45–46; of Rorty, vii, viii; Rorty on the world becoming more pragmatic, xxii; Russell on, 32–33, 50; on science, 34; and subjective-objective distinction, 50; on test of utility as retrospective, 56; truth of pragmatist view of truth, xxvii–xxviii; as way of getting out from under Platonism, 49, 51

"Pragmatism and Romanticism" (Rorty), xxvi

progress: Dewey on, 56; intellectual, 15, 40; James on, 6, 52; moral, xxii, 56; Nietzsche on, 10; Platonism on, 21; political, 56; pragmatism on, 57; romanticism on, 6–7, 21; Rorty on, xxii, 5, 15, 18; slow rate of, 47

psychoanalysis, xvii, xviii

Public Access (Bérubé), x

Quine, Willard Van Orman, xviii, 12, 24

Ramsey, Frank, 26

rationality: analytic philosophers on irrationalists, 32; beginnings of scientific, 20; Brandom's paradigm for rational inquiry, 41; Christianity and, 56; coherence of belief in, 48; Davidson's account of belief and, 38; distinguishing good from bad reasons as, 36; Hegel attempts to combine historicism with rationalism, 54; in jigsaw puzzle

philosophy (*continued*)
view of human situation, 47;
language and, viii, xxiii, xxv, 4,
15; as making acceptable moves
within a set of social practices,
15, 25; mathematics seen as
paradigm for rational thought,
44; philosophy seen as arbiter
of, 60; rational interlocutors,
52; rational standards, 49; relativization of, 62; social-practice
conception of, 55; transcultural, 62; two types of, 53. *See also*
reason

Rawls, John, xviii
Raz, Joseph, 26
realism, xxviii
reason: communicative versus
subject-centered conceptions
of, 54–55; Enlightenment
deification of, 7, 45, 53, 54;
game of giving and asking
for reasons, 36; Habermas on
"others" to, 52; imagination's
priority over, 9, 15, 25, 45,
55, 58; romanticism seen as
substituting inspiration for, 49;
rule of, 58; as social practice,
4, 46, 54; as truth-tracking
faculty, 52, 53, 60; what counts
as a good reason, 52–53; works
within the human world, 9. *See
also* rationality
relativism: analytic philosophers'
criticism of, 32–34; cultural,
53; postmodern relativists,
24–25, 33; relativization of
rationality, 62; Rorty associated
with, vii; social-practice conception of rationality and, 55
religion: as alternative source of

truth, 52; mysticism, 21, 52;
Nietzsche on, 25; questions of
science and, 44; versus secularism, xxviii; theology, 24, 59
representationalism: antiempiricist
view versus, 13; in Cartesian
picture of mind, 14; Davidson's account of belief versus,
38; in empiricism, 11, 12;
giving up talk about mental
representations, 39; pragmatist
anti-representationalism, ix;
progress as increased accuracy
of representations for, 18; repudiation of, 45
romanticism: Berlin on, 46,
48–49, 52; breaks back of
Platonism, 46; combining pragmatism with, 61–62; Hegel as
first philosopher to see significance of, 44; on imagination, 7,
13, 45, 56; notion of objective
criteria undermined by, 48–49;
as philosophy of hope, 57;
pragmatism compared with,
45–46; on "prison-house of
language," 53–54; on progress,
6–7, 21; and quarrel between
philosophy and poetry, 7, 24;
romantic poets, xxix, 7, 9, 31;
seeing it as substituting inspiration for reasoning, 49; and
subjective-objective distinction,
50; as way of getting out from
under Platonism, 49, 51; when
it elevates private insight over
public justifiability, 52
Rorty, Richard: academic progress
of, xviii; air of intellectual
insouciance, xviii, xx; analytic
philosophy and, xvii–xviii; *Con-*

sequences of Pragmatism, xxvii–
xxviii; *Contingency, Irony, and
Solidarity,* xvi; Derrida seminar
of, xv, xvii; "Determinacy
Debate" with Hirsch, xix–xx,
xxi; "The Fire of Life," 65–66;
Freud seminar of, xvii; Heidegger seminar of, x–xvi, xxiv;
"How Relevant Is 'Postmodern'
Philosophy to Politics?," ix;
iconicity resisted by, xv, xvii; on
interesting writers, xxi; on the
ironist, xxiv; on keeping a civil
conversation going, xvi–xvii,
xx; logocentrism of, 65; *Mirror
of Nature,* 64–65; on modesty,
xxix; paradox in philosophical
and political life of, xxi–xxii;
on post-Philosophical society,
xxvii–xxviii; "Pragmatism
and Romanticism," xxvi;
on progress, xxii, 5, 15, 18;
quintessence of Rortyism, ix;
read a lot, 63–64; rhetoric of,
viii–ix, xxvi–xxix; on romantic
poets secularizing the world,
xxix; seen as postmodernist-
nihilist-antifoundationalist-
poststructuralist-sophist-
relativist, vii–viii; as thinking in
both analytic and Continental
traditions, xviii; as without
disciples, xv; words mattered
for, 63; writing style of, vii
Russell, Bertrand: aspiration to
universalist grandeur, 34; versus
Bergson, 24; Heidegger contrasted with, 32; on historicism,
45; hoped to make things clearer, xx–xxi, 28; hopes to retain
Kant as model for philosophy,

44–45; on knowledge, 33, 40;
on logical analysis, 60, 61; on
logical form, 27, 38; on logic as
essence of philosophy, 45; on
philosophy's task, 48; on Plato
on what makes human beings
special, 30; on pragmatism,
32–33, 50; in quest for direct
awareness, 21; requirement for
philosophical analysis of, 37;
theory of descriptions of, 26–
28, 30–31; on truth, 38; versus
Wittgenstein, 64
Ryerson, James, xviii

Schiller, F. C. S., 32
Schiller, Friedrich, 8, 9, 47
science: conflict with theology,
24; corpuscularian natural, 44;
derives from novelty, 5; history
replacing in a culture that had
given up Platonism, 59; literature and the arts replacing, 58;
Marxism's claim to be scientific,
56; nature of scientific theories,
18; Nietzsche on seeing it
through optic of art, 18, 19; in
philosophical supernarrative,
59; philosophy as, 32, 38–39;
philosophy of science, 47;
philosophy seen as queen of
the sciences, 60; physics, ix,
32, 49, 65; pragmatism on, 34;
questions of religion and, 44;
as social practice, 46; talking
about mind and language in
ways consistent with, 35. *See
also* cognitive science
secularization, xxvi, xxviii, xxix,
24, 44
Sellars, Wilfrid: on awareness as

Sellars, Wilfrid (*continued*)
linguistic affair, 12; on Cartesian picture of the mind, 14,
17; in debates within analytic
philosophy, 25; guides in
rediscovery of historicism, 45;
as narrative philosopher, 39;
philosophers who aspire to universalist grandeur versus, 39; on
prelinguistic awareness, 17–18;
Rorty draws from, 11
semantics, naturalized, 32
sense perception, 11–12, 20
Shelley, Percy Bysshe: "Defence of
Poetry," xxix, 7, 52; on imagination, 7, 13, 56; Nietzsche
echoes, 8; on poetry as expression of imagination, 7; on poets
as unacknowledged legislators
of the world, xxix, 9, 18
slavery, 47, 58
social construction, 15–16
social norms, xxv, 4, 36, 40
social practice: being imaginative as
having one's novelties incorporated into, 4; bigger and better,
5; comparing past and present,
39; contingency of, 62; as cul-
turally relative, 53; language as,
4, 25, 34, 35–37; mind as, 25,
34, 35–37; nothing intermediate between neurons and, 36–
37; novel, 55–56; organisms
develop, xxiv, 13; rationality as
making acceptable moves within, 15, 25; reason as, 4, 46, 54;
seeking criteria that transcend,
57; social-practice conception
of rationality, 55; universal and
necessary truth contrasted with,

xxi, 43; Wittgensteinians on,
34–37. *See also* language games
Socrates, 7, 8, 58, 59
Solon, 18
Spencer, Herbert, 54
Spinoza, 23, 24, 44
*Structure of Scientific Revolutions,
The* (Kuhn), xvi
subjective-objective distinction, 50

teleology: immanent, 55, 62; Rorty
as antiteleological, xxii
theodicy, 54, 59
theology, 24, 59
theory of descriptions, 26–28,
30–31
Theory Wars of 1980s, xviii–xix
thing-in-itself, 9, 16
thought: Hegel on philosophy as
its time held in, 43, 59, 64;
language and, viii, xxiii, xxv,
4; poetic imagination sets the
bounds for human, 3. *See also*
cognitive science
truth: analytic philosophers on
deniers of, 32; commonly
accepted truths, 2–3; correspondence theory, 38, 46;
Davidson on, 38; justification
and, 52; nondiscursive access
to, 51, 52; philosophy seen as
search for "Truth," viii, xxii;
reason as truth-tracking faculty,
52, 53, 60; unconditional, 30,
34; universal and necessary, xxi,
43, 47–48
Turner, J. M. W., 49
Twilight of the Gods (Nietzsche), 19

unconditionality, 30, 33, 34, 40